THE ATONEMENT
OF GOD

THE ATONEMENT
OF GOD

Building Your Theology on a Crucivision of God

J. D. Myers

RedeemingPress.com

Published by Redeeming Press
Dallas, OR 97338
RedeemingPress.com

ISBN: 978-1-939992-42-0 (Paperback)
ISBN: 978-1-939992-43-7 (Mobi)
ISBN: 978-1-939992-44-4 (ePub)

Learn more about J. D. Myers by visiting RedeemingGod.com

JOIN JEREMY MYERS AND LEARN MORE

Take Bible and theology courses by joining Jeremy at
RedeemingGod.com/join/

Receive updates about free books, discounted books,
and new books by joining Jeremy at
RedeemingGod.com/reader-group/

Take the FREE
Skeleton Church
online course

Join others at
RedeemingGod.com/join/
to get the *Skeleton Church* online course for free

**Get eBooks and theology courses at
RedeemingGod.com/Join/**

Thanks for reading!

Other Books by Jeremy Myers

Nothing but the Blood of Jesus

The Re-Justification of God: A Study of Rom 9:10-24

Adventures in Fishing (for Men)

Christmas Redemption: Why Christians Should Celebrate a Pagan Holiday

Why You Have Not Committed the Unforgivable Sin

The Gospel According to Scripture

The Gospel Dictionary

Books in the *Close Your Church for Good* Series

Preface: Skeleton Church

Vol. 1: The Death and Resurrection of the Church

Vol. 2: Put Service Back into the Church Service

Vol. 3: Church is More than Bodies, Bucks, & Bricks

Vol. 4: Dying to Religion and Empire

Vol. 5: Cruciform Pastoral Leadership

All books are available at Amazon.com

Learn about each title at the end of this book

For René Girard.
You helped me see my heart in Scripture.

ACKNOWLEDGMENTS

It would be impossible to write a book without the encouragement, support, and input of my wife, Wendy. I often say that she is the inspiration for my theology and my ideas, but this is a vast understatement. She has what I call "intuitive theology." She might not read and study as much as I do, but she doesn't need to spend her time on such things because she intuitively knows the heart of God better than anyone I have ever met. I know that the following statement will get misunderstood, but I am going to write it anyway: If you want to know what God thinks about something, just ask Wendy.

I also want to thank my three daughters, Taylor, Selah, and Kahlea. They don't fully understand exactly what I do, but every time they see my name on a book, they say, "Daddy! You wrote a book? That is *so* cool!" I am glad I can still be cool to my daughters. They are also beginning to ask theological questions at the dinner table, which excites me to no end.

A big thank you goes to Sam Riviera. He has been a friend and an encouragement to me for many years, and an active participant on my blog at RedeemingGod.com. Though I became a

Christian at a young age, Sam introduced me to Jesus when I was in my late 30s. I am forever grateful.

A team of volunteers helped proofread and edit this book. I want to thank them as well. I specifically want to mention Jennifer Lodine-Chaffey, Deidre Havrelock, Kevin Johnson, Nizam Khan, John Kuhne, Pam Wilsey, Vaughn Bender, Ray Turner, Ty Dunbar, Michael Wilson, and David. Since none of them read the entire book before it was published, any errors that remain are still mine.

Finally, I want to thank you. Yes, *you*. Thank you for reading this book at a time when most people don't read books at all, much less read books on theology. The process of researching and writing this book transformed my theology to look more like Jesus, and I trust something similar will happen to you as you read it. Don't say I didn't warn you!

TABLE OF CONTENTS

PREFACE

There are numerous reasons many bible-believing Christians view God as being violent, angry, and vengeful toward sin. Another whole book would be required to survey these reasons and explain the various texts from Scripture which are used to defend the idea of such a God. I am in the process of writing such a book, but at the time of writing this, that other book is only about half-way done, and it contains over 200,000 words (a typical 200-page book contains about 50,000 words). Furthermore, during the five years I have been working on that writing project, my thinking about the violence of God in Scripture and my approach to understanding the violent texts in the Bible have changed and evolved. So the book on the violence of God needs serious editing and refining if it is ever to see the light of day. This process is further impeded by the fact that writing is not my full-time job. I keep waiting for one of my books to become a "best seller" or for some "patron" to finance my writing so that I can spend more time studying, writing, and publishing, but I am not holding my breath on either account. Ha!

In the meantime, shorter books like this one will serve to solidify my thinking on the subjects related to the violence of God, while at the same time (I hope) introduce you to some of the concepts and ideas that will find their way into the future volume(s) on the violence of God. Toward that end, I value your feedback on the ideas in this book. You can provide your feedback by leaving comments on various articles at RedeemingGod.com. By joining my online discipleship group at Redeeming God.com/join/, you will not only gain access to future books and online courses, but will also be able to contact me directly by email.

The way my writing process works, I usually publish my ideas first on my website for feedback and interaction with the community of readers there. These ideas get refined and clarified through the comments, questions, suggestions, and objections of the people there. While I interact with my online community in this way, I start to put some of the revised ideas down on paper for future publication, until these ideas eventually coalesce into a book like the one you are reading now.

So if you would like to join my online discipleship group to take my online courses and participate in my process of writing books, please join me at RedeemingGod.com/join/. If you simply want to receive information about my past, present, and future books, you can join me at RedeemingGod.com/readergroup/. Either way, you will receive several free eBooks from me, so whichever group you join, I can't wait to see you there!

FOREWORD

The cross of Christ is the only gateway to knowledge.
–Simone Weil

The crucifixion of Jesus is central to all of Christian theology. It is on the cross where Jesus most fully reveals God to us. It is through the cross that Jesus accomplished everything related to our salvation. While we must never downplay the importance of the resurrection of Jesus (cf. 1 Cor 15:14-17), we cannot get to the resurrection without going through the crucifixion, and we can only understand the significance of the resurrection if we first grasp what Jesus accomplished in the crucifixion. We must focus on the crucified King as the beginning, middle, and end of all Christian theology (1 Cor 2:2).

The crucifixion of King Jesus is also central to Christian living. The cross shows us how we are to follow Jesus and what we are to focus on in life (Matt 16:24-26). If we get the cross wrong, we get life wrong as well. For this reason, there is a direct correlation between a widespread misunderstanding about the crucifixion of Jesus and the way Christians are often perceived in the world today. One primary reason that Christians are perceived by many in the world today as mean, hateful, bigoted, rude, and angry is because we are unconsciously reflecting a view of the crucifixion that contains a mean, hateful, bigoted, rude, and angry god in the background.

So for the sake of Christian living and theology, it is critical to understand why Jesus went to the cross, what He accomplished on the cross, and what role God the Father played in Jesus' death on the cross.

Let me begin with a disclaimer: I know from past experience that there will be many who take great offense to what I write here. They will say I am ignorant of the Scriptures, that I am ignoring key texts which seem to refute my view, that I don't include enough Scriptural support for my views, and that I don't interact adequately enough with the scholars and theologians who have a differing view. To all these accusations, I say, "Guilty as charged."

Am I ignorant of the Scriptures? Of course! Who among us dares call himself an expert? Twenty years ago I thought I had all the answers. Now, the more I study, the more I realize how little I know.

Am I ignoring key texts or points from key authors which seem to refute my view? Certainly! However, this is not because I am afraid of these texts or have purposefully ignored these authors in my study. Since the crucifixion of Jesus is central to everything, there is simply no room to discuss *most* of the key texts in this debate or deal with even a small fraction of the authors who have written on it. Furthermore, any text which is frequently used to defend or support a particular atonement theory can also be used to defend or support any other atonement theory. So rather than arguing about which texts defend which theory, a better approach is to talk about *how* any particular text can be used to support the various theories, and then ask ourselves *which* of these textual meanings best fits within the overall context of Scripture. Obviously, a study of each particular text in this fashion is well beyond the scope of this book.

By the end of this book, my goal is not to get you to agree with me, but to invite you to study these issues along with me. In the end, it may not be quite as important to know exactly *how* the crucifixion worked as it is to know *that* it works. As long as we can all agree that the historical reality of the death and resurrection of Jesus accomplished our redemption, the debates about *how* He accomplished this are of secondary importance and need not divide us. We can be in unity on the fact of the atonement, even if we disagree on the various theories of how it worked. This reminder from C. S. Lewis is appropriate:

> The central Christian belief is that Christ's death has somehow put us right with God and given us a fresh start. Theories as to how it did this are another matter. A good many different theories have been held as to how it works; what all Christians are agreed on is that it does work. I will tell you what I think it is like. … A man can eat his dinner without understanding exactly how food nourishes him. A man can accept what Christ has done without knowing how it works: indeed, he certainly would not know how it works until he has accepted it.
>
> We are told that Christ was killed for us, that His death has washed out our sins, and that by dying He disabled death itself. That is the formula. That is Christianity. That is what has to be believed. Any theories we build up as to how Christ's death did all this are, in my view, quite secondary: mere plans or diagrams to be left alone if they do not help us, and, even if they do help

us, not to be confused with the thing itself. All the same, some of these theories are worth looking at.[1]

As with most things C. S. Lewis writes, I could not agree more. So let us begin our study by looking at the various theories of the atonement.

One final note before we begin: This book sometimes capitalizes "God" while at other times leaving it uncapitalized as "god." This is intentional. When I capitalize God, I am referring to the God of Scripture as revealed in Jesus Christ. When I use the uncapitalized "god" I am referring to one of the false portrayals of god that are often found in other religions or in some versions of Christianity. This will hopefully enable you to better understand what I am writing, while at the same time help bring your understanding of God in line with His full revelation in Jesus Christ.

---

[1] C. S. Lewis, *Mere Christianity* (New York: Collier, 1952), 54-56.

PART I:
FOUR VIEWS ON THE ATONEMENT

There are numerous views on the atonement. The person who seeks to understand the atonement will likely become quickly overwhelmed by the vast array of atonement views, and the various names and descriptions by which these views are taught. It would impossible to properly summarize and explain *all* the atonement views along with their subtle differences and perspectives. So in Part I of this book, I have sought to summarize and explain the four most common views of the atonement. I chose these four views because they also tend to represent many of the less common views as well. Chapter 1 will look at three of the more popular views in church history during the past 1000 years or so, while Chapter 2 will look at the view which was prominent for the first 1000 years and which is seeing a significant comeback in our modern era.

Before we look at these views, it might be wise to define the word "atonement." Lots of pastors and theologians like to define atonement by saying it means "at-one-ment." That is, atonement is how we become "one" again with God. According to this definition, sin causes a division between us and God, and atonement is how that division is healed so that we regain unity, or "at-one-ment" with God again.

I don't mind this sort of explanation *too* much, but I think it gives the wrong impression about atonement and so sets the whole discussion off on the wrong foot. To say that atonement brings humanity back into unity with God implies that there was a disunity or division between God and humanity that needed to be mended. This division or separation is usually thought to be the result of sin. God, we are told, is so holy and righteous that He cannot be in the presence of sin or even look upon it, and so because we are sinners God separated Himself from us until the sin issue was taken care of in Jesus Christ.

I have major difficulties when atonement teachings are presented this way. From Genesis 3 onward, I do not ever see that God has separated Himself from humanity because of sin. As we will see later in this book, if there was ever any separation between God and humans because of sin, the separation was one-sided: humans fled from God; God never fled from humans. We left God; He did not leave us. Despite our feelings, there was never any chasm or gap between God and humans that needed to be crossed. Sin makes us *feel* like God has abandoned and forsaken us, but the truth is that He has never done so.

I hope to make all of this clear in the following pages. In my view, there is a reconciliation of a broken relationship in God's work of atonement, but it is not to restore a broken unity between God and man, but rather to show us that He has never left us or forsaken us in the first place. There was always unity with God. God was always with us and among us. But we failed to see it. In Jesus, God made it clear what He has always been doing for all humans throughout all of history.

So the atonement is a reconciliation. It is a restoration. It is agreement and concord and fellowship. But it is not God finally doing something about sin so that He can move back toward us. No, it is God finally showing us that He has never left us or forsaken us, but has always been walking with us in our pain and suffering and rebellion. The atonement is not God bringing us back into "at-one-ment" with Him, but showing us that He has always been "at-one-ment" with us. I am not opposed to the "at-one-ment" idea, as long as we recognize that it is not something new in our relationship with God, but is something that has always been true, though we did not recognize it.

The following two chapters will hopefully make this more clear. Chapter 1 will look at three common views of the atonement which indicate a change in God's relationship with humanity. All three views indicate that God was in some sense angry with mankind because of sin, but came to forgive and love humans through the death of Jesus. This will be followed by Chapter 2 which looks at a fourth view of the atonement. This fourth view reveals that God has not changed in His love for mankind. He has always loved and always will. Chapter 2 will show that while the atonement does restore the relationship between God and man, this restoration does not occur through a warlike or violent revolution, but occurs through a divine revelation about God and mankind.

CHAPTER 1

THREE COMMON VIEWS ON THE ATONEMENT

Before we look at the view of the atonement I hold, we will briefly consider three of the other common views of the atonement, beginning with the most prominent view of all, the Penal Substitutionary view.

PENAL SUBSTITUTION VIEW OF THE ATONEMENT

This view goes by various names. Sometimes it is referred to as the Satisfaction theory, the Vicarious Sacrificial theory, the Retributive Justice theory, the Governmental theory, or the Blood Atonement theory. Each of these terms could be pulled out to represent their own unique position on the atonement, but for the sake of space, they are all being lumped together here, and will be referred to by the most commonly occurring title: the Penal Substitution view. This theory is currently the most widely held theory of the atonement in modern Western Christianity. We must hasten to add, however, that the Penal Substitution view has not been the most common view throughout all of church history, nor is it the most common view of the worldwide church today. Few Eastern Christian traditions hold to the Penal Substitutionary view of the atonement. So while Penal Substitution may be the majority view in modern, Western theology, it is a minority view when the entire, historical, worldwide church is taken into consideration. Nevertheless, because this view is relatively common in modern Western Christianity, it is the view (other than the Non-Violent view) that will receive the most attention in this book.

The Penal Substitution view of the atonement was initially developed by a medieval theologian named Anselm (1033-1109), and then later refined by various Reformers such as John Calvin (1509-1564). The Penal Substitutionary view of the atonement has beliefs and practices of the medieval feudal system as its foundation, such as the feudalistic conceptions of honor, authority, sanctions, and reparation.[1] In this system, when a feudal lord's honor was damaged, this damage created a debt which must be repaid. The basic idea of Penal Substitution is that all sin is a moral affront to God's righteousness and honor. Moreover, since God is an eternal being, all sin is an eternal offense. God, because of His justice, cannot simply ignore sin, for this would be unjust. Yet since sin is an eternal affront, the punishment for sin must also be eternal. As the offender, humanity is required to suffer this eternal punishment, which can only be accomplished through eternal torment in hell. God, however, is not only just; He is also loving, and does not desire for people to spend eternity in hell. Therefore, God arranged a way for the eternal debt of sin to be satisfied by oth-

---

[1] Walter Wink, *The Human Being: Jesus and the Enigma of the Son of Man* (Minneapolis: Fortress, 2002), 105.

er means: through the death of Jesus Christ. Since Jesus is God incarnate, He is able to pay the eternal debt of sin by substituting Himself to suffer and die in the place of humanity. In the eternal death of Jesus, the eternal debt of sin is paid. In the substitutionary death of Jesus, the justice of God is satisfied, thereby allowing God to focus His love upon humanity.

As can be seen, "Penal Substitution" is a good term for this view. Penal refers to punishment, and Substitution refers to how Jesus substituted Himself for the punishment that was due to come upon humanity. The various other terms for this view tend to place emphasis on one aspect or another of this view. As the Satisfaction theory, it refers to how the wrath of God was satisfied by the death of Jesus. When the view is referred to as the Vicarious Sacrificial theory, the emphasis is on the sacrifice of Jesus in the place of humanity. When the view is referred to as Retributive Justice, the emphasis is on the justice of God and how God's justice requires punishment upon sinners to remain just. When it is referred to as the Governmental theory, the emphasis is upon the rule of God as the king and judge of the universe. In this view, sin cannot simply be overlooked or forgiven if God is going to abide by the rules of His own government. And when the view is referred to as the Blood Atonement theory, the emphasis is specifically placed upon the shed blood of Jesus being the necessary requirement for the forgiveness of sins.

There will, of course, be numerous objections from people who hold any of the views listed above that their view has not been properly explained, defined, and defended, or that their view should not be lumped together with Penal Substitution. I agree. Each view summarized above should be placed within its own category and given numerous pages of explanation, biblical defense, and quotes from theologians and Bible scholars who hold that particular view. But this chapter is only a brief examination of atonement theories.

Though the Penal Substitution view is the most common view in modern Western Christian theology, it is full of fatal flaws. René Girard says that "this line of reasoning has done more than anything else to discredit Christianity in the eyes of people of goodwill in the modern world."[2] And though Walter Wink says that there are numerous good elements in all other views of the atonement, "The blood-atonement theory is beyond being salvaged."[3] I would not state things quite so strongly, though I do believe that the Penal Substitution view of the atonement is far from being an accurate representation of what Jesus revealed and accomplished on the cross.

Though many do not realize it, the basic logic of Penal Substitution was also the common view of the average religious person in the days of Jesus. Most people in the days of Jesus (as now) believed that God was angry at sinners and that God's honor and justice demanded substitutionary blood sacrifices to satisfy and appease God's wrath toward sin. Such a view of God was popular then (as now) because it fits within the human preconceived notion that God is angry with us about our sin and demands that we somehow pay Him for our numerous affronts to His righteousness and holiness.

But this was not the view of Jesus. To the contrary, through His life and teachings, Jesus sought to deliver the world from such a view of God. Jesus consistently and repeatedly challenged this view. As a result, the religious people sought to kill

---

[2] René Girard, *Things Hidden Since the Foundation of the World*, trans., Stephen Bann and Michael Metteer (Stanford, CA: Stanford University Press, 1987), 182.

[3] Wink, *The Human Being*, 110.

Jesus, which they accomplished through His crucifixion. In other words, the views of the religious people who crucified Jesus had much in common with the Penal Substitution view, and they crucified Jesus *precisely* because His teachings and ministry posed a serious challenge to their view. Jesus fully repudiated their political-religious-judicial perspective about God and sin, and was crucified as a result.

What did Jesus teach instead? Through His ministry, teachings, parables, actions, and miracles, Jesus taught that God had nothing but love for all people, that God freely forgives all people of all their sins, that the sacrificial system was not needed to gain God's forgiveness, that God did not desire the blood of bulls and goats in order to love or forgive, that the temple was not God's sacred space, that the priesthood was not the divinely-ordained mediator between God and men, and that God was just as much in love with our enemies as He was with us. The religious people then (as now) could not handle such a dismantling of their entire theological framework, and so killed Jesus. They didn't kill Jesus simply because they thought Jesus was wrong. No, they killed Him because they viewed Jesus as a blasphemer who directly challenged the honor and holiness of God, and their theology demanded that blasphemers like Jesus be put to death. The honor of God had to be defended. So while we often say that Jesus died for sin, it might be more accurate to say that Jesus died for religion. It was not sin that killed Jesus, but religion. Jesus was killed "in the name of God" by those who sought to protect God's honor and righteousness against the "blasphemous" and "heretical" teachings of Jesus.

It is not surprising, therefore, that those who hold to the Penal Substitutionary view of the atonement today also feel that it is okay for God to kill His enemies and for God's people to do whatever is necessary to defend God's honor and stand against all attacks on God's righteousness. Though people today may not directly kill someone "in the name of God," they do often call for wars against "God's enemies," and they may threaten the livelihood and character of those who believe or behave in ways that are labeled as "sinful" or "wrong." They may even call into question the condition of the eternal soul of those who do not believe in Penal Substitution, or at least accuse them of heresy. Such an approach is similar to the approach used by the religious people who put Jesus on the cross.

Ironically then, it is actually the Penal Substitution view of the atonement which is an affront to the character and honor of God. The Penal Substitution theory of the atonement presents God as a being who created people with free will, then put them in a place where there was a forbidden fruit, knowing full well that they would eat of it. When they did eat from the forbidden tree, He became so angry at them for eating what He told them not to eat (even though He put the fruit within their reach), He was forced to condemn them to death, not just physically, but for all eternity. Due to the sin in the garden, God condemned all people to burn in hell forever. But since God also loved people so much, He created a way to escape this punishment. How? He sent His one and only Son to die a bloody and horrible death in our place.

In this way, Penal Substitution portrays "God as a cruel and unforgiving patriarch, unable to love as a decent parent should, trapped in his own rules that force him to commit a ghastly crime. In that view it is God who needs forgiveness, not us!"[4]

So to summarize, Penal Substitution says this: God loves us. But we sinned. God hates sin. Sin requires punishment. That

---

[4] Ibid., 106.

punishment is death. Not just physical death, but eternal death. But remember, God loves us! So He sent Jesus to be punished in our place. Now God can truly love us again. The basic idea is that while God does love us, sin is in the way of that love. The way God dealt with sin is by sending His innocent Son to die for us in our place.

> Is this God's plan, to become a human being and die, so that God won't have to destroy us instead? Is it God's prescription to have Jesus suffer for sins he did not commit so God can forgive the sins we do commit?[5]

Yet "this interpretation appears contrary to both the spirit and letter of the Gospels."[6] Imagine a similar situation in any other context. Consider what we would think of a father who, during World War II, had given up his only child to Adolph Hitler so that he might torture and murder him, in exchange for a promise to release all the Jewish prisoners in all the concentration camps. Would such a father be considered a hero or a monster? I suspect that while we would *want* to say he had done a good thing, few of us could bring ourselves to believe it.

> We can hardly imagine God planning the suffering and death of one innocent as the condition of releasing guilty others. And it would be worse if we could do so, for a God about whom this is the truth is a God we could hardly love and worship.[7]

---

[5] S. Mark Heim, *Saved From Sacrifice: A Theology of the Cross* (Grand Rapids: Eerdmans, 2006), xi.

[6] René Girard, *I See Satan Fall Like Lightning* (Maryknoll, NY: Orbis, 2001), 21.

[7] S. Mark Heim, "Why Does Jesus' Death Matter?" http://www.religion-online.org/showarticle.asp?title=2138 Last Accessed January 9, 2014.

It is argued, however, that the situation with God is different. Penal Substitution proponents say that it is not as though Jesus was an unwilling victim as in the example above. Jesus came willingly to suffer and die. So the picture is not so much of a cruel and sadistic man torturing his son for the sake of others, but instead of a heroic man jumping on a grenade or stepping in front of a bullet for the sake of his friends.

While I completely agree that this is much closer to the picture presented by Penal Substitution, it is, however, undeniable that in Penal Substitution, it is God who threw the grenade or shot the gun. So while Jesus is heroic, Penal Substitution makes Him into a hero who saves us from His angry Father.

Even here, of course, there will be objections to the portrayal of God as an angry Father. "God is not angry at humans," people will say. "God loves humans. Instead, God is angry at sin. God is righteous and holy, and justice must be served." They go on to explain that in order to rescue sinful humanity, a perfect and innocent sacrificial substitute is necessary to pay the penalty for sin. In Penal Substitution, God is presented as merciful and loving, but also just. And since sin demands payment, someone had to pay, and since humans could not, God stepped in and, through the death of Jesus, paid the debt of sin.

I will admit that this initially sounds very clean and tidy … as long as you do not really think about the words and ideas being used. It is said that God is merciful and forgiving, but justice demands payment for the debt of sin. When you actually begin to think about the basic definitions of these words, you come to realize that God cannot be both *merciful and forgiving,* while at the same time allow *justice to demand payment for the debt of sin.* Why not? The two sets of ideas are mutually exclusive.

If the death of Jesus satisfies the debt of human sin which was owed to God, how then can God be said to be merciful and forgiving? If the debt is paid, mercy and forgiveness are meaningless. If mercy and forgiveness are extended, then the payment of a debt is not required. In other words, there can be *either* the payment of debt, *or* mercy extended; but not both. Payment and mercy are, by definition, mutually exclusive.

Some argue, however, that God's payment of the debt *is* mercy, since although a debt is usually paid by the guilty party, God is the one who pays the debt Himself in the death of Jesus. But it is a queer sort of mercy which requires a debt to be paid by oneself to oneself on behalf of a third party. If there really was a debt owed to God, and He decided to pay Himself to cancel the debt to Himself, He doesn't actually need to pay Himself at all. He can just forgive the debt (which, incidentally, is exactly what He did, as we will see later in this book). The only way in which God could be seen to be merciful in paying the debt for mankind's sin by killing Jesus is if the debt to be paid was not due to God, but to someone or something else entirely. This is another view, the "Ransom View," which will be discussed near the end of this chapter.

Another reason to reject the Penal Substitution view is that it relies upon the pagan sacrificial beliefs that blood sacrifices are needed to appease the wrath of God. But God does not need, want, or desire the death of bulls and goats in order to forgive (See Appendix 1 for a discussion of Hebrews 9:22). Instead, Jesus revealed that God is not angry at sin and freely forgives without any need for blood sacrifice. Those who thought that God required blood sacrifice were those who crucified Jesus in the name of God. Those who today believe that God demands blood sacrifice do not side with God and Jesus regarding the crucifixion, but side with those who crucified

Jesus to appease an angry God. The Penal Substitution view of the atonement reintroduces "sacral violence back into the heart of Christianity. Jesus is the scapegoat on whom the sins of the world are laden. He is driven out and killed in a charade of justice that means regression to the sacrificial mentality from which Jesus sought to free people."[8]

> The most familiar form of the atonement doctrine ... supposes that a wrathful God demanded that a victim pay in blood for human sin—like the animals that died in the atonement sacrifices at the Jewish Temple—and that God chose to take a human form and pay for the sin "Himself." It is an understandable doctrine, given the religious and cultic background against which early Christian thought was first forming. But the doctrine is not only logically incoherent; it is morally and theologically inadequate as well.[9]

There is one final reason to reject Penal Substitution, and it is more of a practical reason than theological. Though many may not realize it, the Penal Substitutionary view of the atonement has led countless masses of people to abandon Christianity and reject God as worthy of worship. "What is wrong with this God," says Walter Wink, "whose legal ledgers can be balanced only by means of the death of an innocent victim?"[10]

> The God whom Jesus revealed as no longer vengeful, but unconditionally loving, who needed no satisfaction by blood—this God

---

[8] Wink, *The Human Being*, 106.

[9] Gil Bailie, *Violence Unveiled: Humanity at the Crossroads* (New York: Crossroad, 2013), 37.

[10] Walter Wink, *The Powers That Be: Theology for a New Millennium* (New York: Galilee, 1998), 87.

of mercy was changed by the church into a wrathful God whose demand for blood atonement leads to God's requiring his own Son's death on behalf of us all. The nonviolent God of Jesus becomes a God of unequaled violence, since God not only allegedly demands the blood of the victim who is most precious to him, but holds humanity accountable for a death that God both anticipates and requires. Against such an image of God the revolt of atheism is an act of pure religion![11]

It is a shocking idea to think that atheism is a Godly reaction to the ungodly violent portrayal of the God of Penal Substitution.

Eric Siebert also has difficulties with the Penal Substitution view. He writes this:

Despite its popularity, penal substitutionary atonement is problematic at a variety of levels. I do not consider it an appropriate way to understand the significance of Jesus' death. ... Death was the tragic—though predictable—result of Jesus' life, a life committed to inaugurating the kingdom of God, God's reign of peace and justice, on earth.[12]

The Penal Substitution view of the atonement, though popular in modern Western Christianity, does not align with the God revealed in Jesus Christ and must therefore be rejected. Far from adequately portraying the way God truly is, the god of Penal Substitution is a violent, vindictive, and unforgiving god who operates in direct contrast to the character and nature of

---

[11] Ibid., 89. Cf. similar statements made in Walter Wink, *Engaging the Powers: Discernment and Resistance in a World of Domination* (Minneapolis: Fortress, 1992), 149.

[12] Eric A. Seibert, *Disturbing Divine Behavior: Troubling Old Testament Images of God* (Minneapolis: Fortress, 2009), 198.

Jesus Christ. Therefore, Penal Substitution is an inadequate view of the atonement.[13]

THE MORAL INFLUENCE VIEW

The Moral Influence view of the atonement is sometimes referred to as the Exemplary Love view. The basic idea with this view is that the death of Jesus did not actually *accomplish* anything related to removing sin, placating God, defeating the devil, or securing forgiveness for humanity. Instead, the death of Jesus on the cross provides the supreme example of what it means to love others. In a world that is filled with violence and selfishness, Jesus Christ showed a better way to live, and He did this not only with His life, but also with His death. The death of Jesus on the cross teaches us to lay down our lives for others, and to live in a self-sacrificial way toward others. Jesus led the way toward this new kind of life by giving us the ultimate example to follow.

The great strength of the Moral Influence or Exemplary Love view is that nobody can object to the idea that Jesus provided humanity the greatest example of what it means to live with self-sacrificial love toward others. Numerous statements by Jesus and various New Testament writers clearly support the idea that Jesus wants us to follow His example in laying down our lives for others as the ultimate expression of love for them (cf. John 3:16; 13:34-35; 15:13; 1 John 4:10).

---

[13] After writing this section, I found an article by Greg Boyd which outlines 10 problems with the Penal Substitution view of the atonement. You can read it here: http://reknew.org/2015/12/10-problems-with-the-penal-substitution-view-of-the-atonement/ Last Accessed December 13, 2015.

In some presentations of this view, the incarnation and crucifixion are not so much the ways God dealt with sin, but are
simply ways for God to show that He was with us in our pain.
The incarnation and crucifixion of Jesus served as revelations
of divine empathy. They showed us that we are not alone.

> Christ did not suffer to satisfy either the wrath of God or ... to
> cancel the sin-content of the whole world, as though weighed in
> some divine balance. He suffered ... to prove the divine love to
> be unalterable in face even of the sin-intractable and pain-bearing
> of the whole world. ... The atoning sacrifice was neither a rescue
> operation nor the rebuilding of a shattered bridge. ... Christ the
> Logos was placing himself in total sharing sympathy with the of-
> ten grueling suffering which man encounters in the hazards of
> growth.[14]

There are several problems with the Moral Influence view.
First, this view does not seem to take into account everything
the Scripture teaches about human slavery to sin, death, and the
devil. If we are truly enslaved to such things, it would seem
that we need more than just an example to follow in order to
break free. Instead, we need a rescuer, a deliverer, a savior. We
need someone to break us out of prison and set us free. Before
we can follow the example of Jesus, we must first be freed
from captivity and slavery.

A second problem is that this view seems to deny the
uniqueness of the revelation of God in Jesus Christ. If Jesus
accomplished nothing more than to provide us with a moral
example to follow, then He is on par with other exemplary
moral and religious leaders throughout all of history. If Jesus is

---

[14] Andrew Elphinstone, *Freedom, Suffering and Love* (London: SCM Press,
1976), 141, 142, 147.

simply an example to follow, then what sets Him apart from other moral, religious teachers such as Zoroaster, Buddha, Krishna, Confucius, or Moses? Wouldn't following their example be just as beneficial as following the example of Jesus?

Finally, if Jesus simply provides an example to follow, then there is little hope for anyone obtaining eternal life. For if Jesus is simply an example, then He did not accomplish our redemption on the cross, and the only avenue for redemption left to us is to work toward the moral excellence of Jesus Christ, which none of us can achieve. If following the example of Jesus was the condition for receiving eternal life, then none would receive eternal life. For this reason, many who hold to the Moral Influence view also hold to some form of universalism. For those who hold this view, the goal of life here and now is then to simply follow the example of Jesus as best we can, for this is how peace and prosperity spreads upon the earth.

In the end, while we must certainly agree that Jesus provides a great example for all people to follow, not only in His life but also in His death on the cross, this view does not say enough about Jesus. Certainly Jesus provided an example to follow, but He did not provide *only* an example. The other atonement views also look to Jesus as an example to follow, but they agree that providing an example to follow is not the *only* reason Jesus came, lived, and died.

So while we do not exactly reject the Moral Influence view of the atonement, we do not adopt it either. Instead, we are able to incorporate this view into whatever other view of the atonement we hold.

THE RANSOM VIEW

There are several forms of the Ransom view of the atonement, and some scholars equate it with the Non-Violent view discussed in the next chapter. But when the two views are understood, it is seen that they have very little in common. The Ransom view is based on the idea that sin creates a debt or ransom which must be paid, and the death of Jesus on the cross was the way it was paid. As a result of paying this ransom, Jesus Christ set free those who were held in bondage by this ransom. The Ransom view is sometimes called the Liberation view, because Jesus liberated those who were in bondage by paying the ransom for their freedom.

The Ransom view is divided into two main groups, and both center on the question about *to whom* the ransom was paid. The first group says that since all sin is primarily a sin against God, the debt of sin must be paid *to God*. When a person holds this particular perspective of the Ransom view, they usually fit within the Penal Substitution view discussed above and incorporate ransom and debt-repayment language into their teaching on the atonement.

The second group says that the ransom is paid to Satan. The argument is that when Adam and Eve sinned, they essentially sold the human race to Satan. God wanted humans to be free, but since Satan held humanity ransom, he required a ransom payment from God. God, by sending Jesus to die, paid the ransom price to Satan so that Satan would set the human captives free. The reason Satan accepted this as payment is because he did not realize that sin and death could not hold Jesus.

Many people believe that the Ransom to Satan view of the atonement was the main view of the church for the first thousand years of Christianity. However, in his book, *Christus Vic-*

tor, Gustaf Aulen shows that the Ransom to Satan view is a misunderstanding and mischaracterization of what the early church taught about the death of Jesus. While it is true that the devil failed to understand that sin and death would not hold Jesus, this should not in any way be understood as God paying a ransom to Satan with the blood of His only Son.

Ransom terminology is popular in many Christian circles because most people in the world have a transactional, economic, judicial mindset about life. This mindset gets carried over into our theology, whereby we think that by getting Adam and Eve to sin, the devil somehow gained the upper hand over God, and so God had to *pay off* Satan, or cancel out the debt that was *owed* to Satan. We think that because of all our sin, mankind has racked up a huge debt which could only be paid with something of supreme value to God. And what could be more valuable than the life of Jesus Christ, God incarnate?

So what can we say about this view? First, it is true that the death of Jesus on the cross defeated sin, death, and the devil and therefore liberated humanity from the bonds of oppression. However, liberation is not the same thing as paying a ransom. While Scripture does refer occasionally to a ransom (Mark 10:45; 1 Tim 2:5-6), such terminology does not automatically imply that there was someone to whom the payment is made. For, as Walter Wink points out,

> When we speak of someone dying for their country [we say they paid the ultimate price, but] we do not envision another to whom their life is paid. When someone is liberated from a concentration camp, no payment is made. People are simply set free. Thus Isai-

ah 35:10—"And the ransomed of the Lord shall return." Again, no payment.[15]

Satan did not get the upper hand over God, nor did God pay off Satan by sending Jesus to die. Jesus can die *for* sin, or even to ransom us *from* sin, without making any sort of payment to anybody. Jesus did pay the ultimate price by giving His life as a ransom for many, but in so doing, He did not pay God or Satan the ransom price. Jesus simply broke into our prison and invited us to follow Him to freedom. Though Jesus did "ransom" us, He did not pay anything to God or Satan. Jesus made no payment. Though humans think in terms of debt and repayment, Jesus, through His life, death, and resurrection, revealed that there is no debt at all. No repayment was necessary because there was never any debt of sin to be repaid.

CONCLUSION

So all three common views of the atonement are deficient when compared to Scripture, theology, and reason. A fourth view is needed, which retains the strengths of these three views while avoiding their weaknesses. This is the view we will consider in the next chapter.

---

[15] Wink, *The Human Being*, 109.

CHAPTER 2

THE NON-VIOLENT VIEW
OF THE ATONEMENT

There are various versions of the Non-Violent view of the atonement. While the *Christus Victor* view is the most common Non-Violent view of the atonement, not all who hold to a Non-Violent view are in full agreement with the details of the *Christus Victor* view. I am one of those. So while I do find myself within the *Christus Victor* camp, I find it easier and better to describe my own view as "the Non-Violent view" of the atonement. Furthermore, describing this view as "Non-Violent" rather than *Christus Victor* makes it more easily understood.

While Non-Violent views of the atonement may not be in the majority today in Western Christianity, various versions of the Non-Violent view were the most dominant views (and possibly the *only* views) for the first 300 years of the church. Non-Violent views of the atonement continued to be in the majority up until at least 1100 A.D. and maybe even until the 16th century when the teachings of the Reformers swept through Europe. Various versions of the Non-Violent view are still the dominant views of most brands of Eastern Christianity. Even Western Christianity is starting to see some shifting in recent years as many pastors, teachers, and scholars now believe that a Non-Violent atonement best presents the full sweep of biblical history and makes the most sense of everything the Bible says about what God was doing in Jesus Christ through the cross.[1] Among these pastors, teachers, and scholars are C. S. Lewis, N. T. Wright, Greg Boyd, Eugene Peterson, Richard Rohr, Marcus Borg, Brian McLaren, Michael Hardin, Derek Flood, Brian Zahnd, Walter Wink, J. Denny Weaver, Brad Jersak, and numerous others. As for myself, though I was taught Penal Substitution in Bible College and Seminary,[2] and though I believed and taught Penal Substitution when I was a pastor, over the past ten years I have become fully convinced of the Non-Violent view of the atonement.

The basic idea of the Non-Violent view of the atonement is that while Jesus did indeed die a violent death on the cross, it was not God who put Jesus there, but humans. Jesus "stepped in front of the bullet," but humanity, not God, held the smoking gun. In this way, the death of Jesus on the cross does not reveal a God who is angry at sin and must punish it through the torturous death of His only Son, but instead reveals a God who has always loved, always forgiven, and always borne the brunt

---

[1] Since Non-Violent views of the atonement encompass so much of biblical history and theology, some are uncomfortable as viewing it as an atonement theory at all, and instead view it as a narrative framework of Scripture. See Derek Flood, *Healing the Gospel: A Radical Vision for Grace, Justice, and the Cross* (Eugene, OR: Cascade, 2012), 41.

[2] I do not remember ever being taught a Non-Violent view of the atonement in Bible College or Seminary. I recently went back and checked my Soteriology notes from both institutions, and was amused/shocked/amazed to discover that while we learned about the Penal Substitution, Moral Influence, and Ransom to Satan views in my classes, we were not taught a Non-Violent view of the atonement. I wonder to this day why they neglected to mention this important view from church history and tradition, especially since many believe that it best represents the full sweep of biblical data.

of our sin on Himself. In dying as He did "for our sin" (or *because* of our sin), He revealed to us once and for all that God is love and in Him there is no violence at all. Though the death of Jesus on the cross was violent, this violence does not reflect divine violence, but human violence. This is why we can call it the Non-Violent atonement.

But the death of Jesus on the cross was much more than the supreme revelation of God's character and human violence. The crucifixion was also the means by which Jesus defeated the oppressive powers of sin, death, and the devil. (This is why some refer to this view as the *Christus Victor* view; Christ was victorious over sin, death, and the devil.) Such things held us captive, and the incarnation of Jesus was a rescue operation to deliver us from this bondage. So the Non-Violent view of the atonement can be viewed through the *Christus Victor* themes of Christ's non-violent victory over sin, death, and the devil.

VICTORY OVER SIN

To understand how Jesus was victorious over sin, we need to understand what sin is (or is not), and specifically, why God tells us not to sin. We can see some of this by looking at the opening chapters of Genesis. In Genesis 1–2, God creates the universe and as the pinnacle of creation, places man and woman in the Garden of Eden to cultivate the plants and tend to the animals. There is also a tree in the garden from which they should not eat of its fruit, lest they die (Gen 2:17). But Adam and Eve eat the forbidden fruit. They commit the world's first sin.

But they do not immediately die. Instead, they hide. They hide themselves from each other by making clothes to hide their nakedness, and they hide themselves from God by avoiding Him when He walks in the garden in the cool of the day (Gen 3:7-8). Why did they hide? Because they were afraid (Gen 3:10). Sin introduced fear into our relationship with God and fear of God causes us to hide from Him. Note that in the Genesis account, after Adam and Eve sin, God still comes to walk with them in the cool of the day. God is not offended or angered by their sin; He did not come into the Garden to punish Adam and Eve. Instead, God came to walk with them. Though they had sinned, He still desired fellowship with sinful humanity. It is Adam and Eve who hide from God, and the first spoken words of sinful humanity in the Bible to God are "I was afraid."

Yet they had no reason to be afraid. Yes, there were disastrous consequences of sin, but these consequences were not a punishment; nor did they come from the supposed anger of God, for God was not angry. This is why nearly every time the angel of the Lord appears to humans in Scripture, the first words out of his mouth are "Do not be afraid." Because of sin, we believe God is angry at us for our sin, but Scripture consistently reveals that God is not angry. The greatest lie of sin is that God is angry at us because of our sin, and that when we sin, we cannot be with God, but must hide from Him.

We have all seen this in our own lives. When we sin, we often feel like God wants nothing to do with us, that He will not hear our prayers, instruct us from Scripture, or bless us for gathering with believers. And so we stop praying, stop reading Scripture, and stop gathering with other Christians. Instead, we wallow deeper into sin. Why? Because in our guilt about sin, we are afraid that God has rejected us for our sin and that God will punish us. This guilt, shame, and fear only leads us deeper into sin.

This is the first and greatest lie of sin, and one of the primary lies that Jesus exposed through His life, ministry, and death on the cross. The truth is that God is not angry at us because of our sin.

What is God's response to our sin? He loves. Period. God loves us in our sin. While we were yet sinners, Christ died for us. Even in the midst of our sin, while we are sinning, God loves us infinitely, enough to send His Son to rescue us from sin. We see this from the very first sin. In the Garden of Eden, though God knew full well what Adam and Eve had done, He went out looking for them, calling for them, to walk with them and be with them (Gen 3:8-9). And even though they had sinned, He still stood with them, told them what the consequences of their sin would be, and even took steps to protect them from the worst of these consequences (Gen 3:17-24). God is not angry with us because of our sin. He never has been angry at us and He never will be.

Even though God is not angry at us for our sin, we can say that God is angry *at sin.* Why? Because sin hurts us. Sin has disastrous, devastating, and destructive consequences, and because God loves us so much, He does not want to see us hurt by sin. Instead, He seeks to protect us from sin. But when we sin, God is not angry at us, but is angry at sin for how it hurts us. His feelings toward us are nothing but love, forgiveness, and friendship. Rather than punish us for sin, God desires to protect us from sin and its consequences.

This leads to the second great lie about sin. We believe that our sin offends and disgusts God. Nothing could be further from the truth. Sin does not offend God. God is not disgusted with us for our sin. Frankly, sin is not that big of a deal to God. Yes, God instructs us to keep away from sin, but this is not because He is disgusted by it, but because we are destroyed by it.

Sin hurts us, and God does not want to see us hurt by sin. Sin controls us, draws us into addiction and destructive habits, and then infects and damages all areas of our lives. Sin destroys our marriage, family, finances, health, and emotional well-being. Adam and Eve hid themselves not only from God, but from each other. They made clothes from fig leaves to cover their nakedness, which means that shame had entered into their relationship. After they sinned, they could not stand before each other fully open, fully honest, and fully revealed. This is what sin does to us in all our relationships and with all our connections to God's creation. God created us to live in perfect harmony with each other and with the plants and animals, but sin destroyed all that. Sin brought disharmony and blame toward others for our sin (Gen 3:12-13). Sin brought difficulties and damage to all areas of life (Gen 3:14-19). Sin brought exile from our home (Gen 3:23-24).

The greatest destructive consequence of sin is that sin brought death, just as God had warned. But the death brought by sin was not simply physical death by old age (though it did bring that). The author of Genesis is intent on showing that sin brought the worst kind of death: sin brought fratricide, murder between brothers when Cain murdered Abel. We will return to this idea below when we look at how Jesus was victorious over death. But before we can get there, it is important to see the third lie about sin, the lie which led to Cain's murder of Abel.

The third great lie about sin is that God requires repayment for sin. After Adam and Eve sinned, God told them that the seed of the woman would bruise the head of the serpent (Gen 3:15). It is likely that Cain and Abel grew up hearing about how good things were in the Garden, and how their parents messed up by eating the forbidden fruit, forcing God to exile them from the Garden. Part of this story would have included

God's promise that Eve's children would crush the head of the serpent that had deceived her, and in so doing, maybe they could get back into the Garden.

So when Cain brings an offering of fruit to God, we can read it as him trying to repay God for the fruit that his parents ate (Gen 4:3). Cain was trying to give back to God the fruit his parents stole. This also explains why Cain's offering was not accepted by God. Cain was trying to repay God for something that did not need to be repaid. He was trying to work off the debt of his parents to God. He was trying to manipulate God into granting him and his family access back into the Garden of Eden. Cain was trying to be the savior of his family. But this is not what God wanted. God wanted Cain and Abel, along with Adam and Eve, to know that they were already accepted, already forgiven, and already loved. There was nothing they needed to do for God in order to get back into God's good graces, for they never left His good graces. The reason they had been cast out of the Garden was not because God was punishing them, but because He was blessing them with death.

How is death a blessing? Death is a blessing for a sinful human being because the only alternative is eternal life in a sinful body. Death is the only way to get rid of sinful flesh and receive a new, perfect, glorious, sinless body.

But Cain misunderstood, as most humans have similarly misunderstood. Cain thought God was angry and that a debt of sin needed to be repaid. So he tried to give God's fruit back to Him. When God saw what Cain was doing and what was in Cain's heart, God warned Cain that such thinking about God's anger and a debt of sin that needed to be repaid would only lead to greater sin. When Cain offered fruit to God, God's response to Cain was, "Sin is crouching at your door, and it will destroy you" (cf. Gen 4:7). The sin that God was warning Cain about was the *religious* sin of trying to make amends with God.

Nevertheless, ever since Cain's offering, people have been trying to give to God what they think He wants so that they can get from God what they want. Cain tried to give God what he thought God wanted so that he could bring his family back into Paradise. Many people today try to give God what they think God wants so that He will give them a good harvest, a happy marriage, a successful business venture, or entrance into heaven. This is the third lie of sin—that we can give something to God in order for Him to love us, forgive us, and accept us back into His family.

So the three great lies of sin are: God is angry with us for our sin, sin disgusts and offends God and so He stays away from us, and God demands repayment for a debt of sin. Seeing these three lies of sin helps us understand how Jesus was victorious over sin. Through His life, teachings, and death on the cross, Jesus exposed all these lies of sin for what they were. Jesus defeated sin by emptying it of its deceitful power over humanity. He taught us and showed us that God is not angry with us about our sin, but has always loved us. He showed us that the reason God wants us not to sin is not because God is disgusted by sin, but because we are damaged and hurt by sin, and God does not want those He loves to be hurt. Furthermore, God showed us in Jesus Christ that there is nothing we can do and nothing He wants us to do in order to repay Him for our sin. There is no debt of sin which is owed to God. He forgives us, loves us, and accepts us freely, by His grace. All of this is what Jesus taught through His life, His ministry, and especially, through His death on the cross. Jesus was victorious over sin by exposing the three main lies of sin.

To understand how Jesus exposed the lies of sin, it is important to also see how Jesus was victorious over death, for sin and death are intimately connected.

VICTORY OVER DEATH

The Non-Violent view of the atonement holds that Jesus not only defeated sin, but also defeated death. And He defeated death in the strangest of ways: He defeated death by dying. Many people believe that Jesus defeated death by rising from the dead. But this is not exactly true. The resurrection proved that sin could not hold Jesus in death. The resurrection was the vindication of Jesus by God against all the accusations that were leveled against Jesus by the religious and political authorities who put Him to death. The resurrection proved that a new age had dawned, that new life had come, that God was now in control of the world. The resurrection proved that death no longer had mastery over the human race. But the resurrection itself did not defeat death. The death of Jesus is what defeated death.

To understand this, we must understand what the Bible means when it talks about death. People sometimes get confused when they hear that Jesus defeated death, for, as everybody knows, all people still die. Shouldn't victory over death lead to no more death? Eventually, it *will* lead to that, but in the interim, we must understand Jesus' victory over death in a different light. The preliminary (and possibly more important) victory over death was in unveiling the power of death. The death of Jesus defeated death by revealing that death was dead. The real victory over death was in revealing to us the emptiness and powerlessness of death.

Let me be more specific: When Jesus defeated death by dying, He was not first and foremost defeating our own personal deaths, but was defeating our enslavement and captivity to the death *of others*. Did you know you were enslaved to the death of others? Most likely, you didn't. But that is because most of humanity still has not grasped the truth that Jesus revealed on the cross through His own death. The truth hidden since the foundation of the world, the truth that we are enslaved and enthralled with death, and specifically, the death of others. To see this truth, let us return once again to the opening chapters of Genesis.

After God creates the heavens and the earth and places Adam and Eve in the garden, God warns Adam not to eat from the Tree of the Knowledge of Good and Evil, lest they die (Gen 2:17; Gen 3:3). But after they eat the forbidden fruit, Adam and Eve do not die. At least, not physically, and not right away. So was God wrong? Was the serpent correct when it told Eve, "You will not surely die" (Gen 3:4)? Well, Adam did eventually die (Gen 5:5), and Eve as well, but in between God's warning about death and Adam's physical death by old age, the Bible introduces us to a much worse form of death: death by murder. And this first murder was the worst kind of murder. It was fratricide, murder between brothers.

One reason that the first murder in human history is fratricide is to show us that all murder is fratricide. All people are brothers and sisters, and so all murder is a murder of a brother or sister. But another reason the first death in Scripture is fratricide is to reveal the power that the death of others holds over all humanity. As indicated earlier, Cain believed it was his responsibility to rescue his family from exile. So he tried to give God's fruit back to Him. Abel, seeing that his older brother was making an offering to God, imitated his brother, and made an offering of his own (Gen 4:4).[3] The text goes on to say that God accepted Abel's offering, but did not accept Cain's. Why? Because Abel was only imitating Cain, but Cain was trying to manipulate God. In essence, God looked at Cain's offering of fruit and said, "I don't want the fruit. You do not understand. I am not angry at you. I do not want offerings. I just want you. I want to live life with you. Go ahead, keep the fruit for yourself. Eat it. Enjoy it. It's yours." But Cain believed that God's justice had been violated, that His honor had been offended, and Cain believed that something must be done to restore God's honor and make the world "right" once again. Cain believed that justice must be served, that order must be re-introduced, and that satisfaction must be made. Most importantly, Cain believed it was *his* responsibility to make things right, to restore order, and to serve justice.

But when Cain saw that Abel imitated him in giving an offering to God, Cain became protective of what he thought was "his." He was the firstborn. He was the first "seed" of his mother, Eve, and therefore it was his right and privilege to be the one about whom God had spoken in Genesis 3:15. Cain wanted to be the one who crushed the serpent's head, restored fellowship with God, and rescued his family from exile. Cain had always assumed that he would be the one to restore his family to the garden. It was his role, his birthright, his respon-

---

[3] It is possible that Abel did not make a blood sacrifice, but rather made an offering to God of live animals from the firstborn of the flock and of the milk ("and of the fat"). Many believe that people were vegetarians at this point in history (cf. Gen 9:2-4), so it would not have occurred to Abel to give meat to God. Some point to Genesis 3:21 as evidence that Abel was following God's example in killing an animal, but not even Genesis 3:21 says that God killed an animal to give "tunics of skin" to Adam and Eve. But none of this matters for the point I am making here.

sibility to rescue and deliver his family. So when Abel imitated Cain and brought an offering to God, Cain thought Abel was making a move to steal the blessing, position, and honor of being the family deliverer. Cain wanted to save his family, and he thought Abel was making a move to steal this honor.

Cain's frustration is only amplified when Abel's offering was accepted by God, while Cain's was not. When this happened, Cain no longer saw Abel as his brother, but as his rival. Cain believed that Abel was trying to steal what belonged to Cain. He thought Abel was trying to become the savior of the family, a position reserved for him alone.

This sense of injustice, of displacement, of rivalry between brothers, is what led to the first murder. God saw the rivalry that was growing in Cain's heart, and warned him that the sin of trying to make amends with God would lead to a greater sin of competing against his brother to make amends with God, and this would lead only to death and destruction (Gen 4:8).

So to protect his position, his role, his legacy, and his rights, Cain murdered Abel (Gen 4:8). Cain didn't like to have a rival, and so he murdered his brother. In this way, God's promise that eating the forbidden fruit would lead to death was fulfilled in the first generation of humans after Adam and Eve were exiled from the Garden of Eden. And it was a murder of brother against brother. This rivalrous murder of brothers began a cycle of contagious violence, murder, and death that spun out of control and enveloped the whole earth.

Cain immediately recognized that as a result of murdering his brother, others would try to murder him. God, in His forgiveness and grace, warned against this sort of retaliation by saying that the murder of Cain will only result in a sevenfold exponential increase in death (Gen 4:15). But within a few verses, Lamech kills a young man for wounding him. Lamech declares that he had more right to kill this young man than Cain had for killing Abel, and so if Cain is to be avenged sevenfold, Lamech will be avenged seventy-sevenfold. This reveals that the exponential increase in the death of others has captivated and enthralled all of humanity. The death that came upon the world was not simply the death of each of us by sickness and old age, but the death of others at our own hand, and out of a sense of murderous rivalry and self-protecting revenge. The death that came upon the world was death by murder, death for revenge, death out of envy and rivalry.

If there is one main theme that binds Genesis 5–11 together, it is death. Genesis 5 contains a long list of people who died. Genesis 6–9 reveals that violence escalated to such a degree and spun so far out of control that it covered the whole earth (Gen 6:5, 13). In the end, all but eight are killed in a flood of death.[4] Genesis 10 reveals the rebuilding of humanity through birth and death, and Genesis 11 shows what this new humanity tries to do to protect itself from future destruction. They embark on an attempt to build a tower that reaches to the heavens (Gen 11:4). If this tower was similar to the Ziggurats found in various places in Mesopotamia, it likely would have had some sort of temple at its peak, in which human sacrifice was a regular occurrence. In an attempt to appease the wrath of the gods, humans made ritualistic human sacrifices to the gods. As sociologist René Girard has pointed out in numerous of his books, human sacrifice developed as a scapegoating ritual where the escalation of murderous rage was controlled by channeling it into one victim. Human sacrifice was the violence of all against

---

[4] A future book I am writing will explain the flood account in more detail, showing why God takes the blame for drowning the whole world in a flood.

one, and served as a means to avoid the contagion of violence of all against all. The point of Genesis 3–11 is to show that sin led to death, and specifically the death of others at our hands. Sin led to murder and violence, and not just any murder or any violence, but the murder of brothers which escalated to an all-consuming contagion of violence that was only arrested through the ritualistic controlled violence of sacrificial religion. When God warned Adam and Eve that sin would lead to death, this is what He had in mind.

Ever since sin entered the world, all of humanity has been controlled and enslaved by death. We are enthralled and en-slaved to the death of the other as a means to save ourselves. The death of the other has been our deliverer. For most of hu-man history, the death of the other has been the savior of the self. We kill others so that we ourselves might live. We look to death to solve all our problems and defeat our enemies and get us what we want. We rationalize death by saying it was "us or them." This is the rationale of murder which is behind every other murder as well.

Most murderers do not think of themselves as murderers, but as vigilantes of justice. Their murder of another person was justified. They were righting a wrong, killing a criminal, or invoking vengeance upon some injustice done to them or their family. Every murderer is able to justify his own murder. All violence is "justifiable." But this justifiable violence leads only to more violence, and as violence escalates out of control, we create scapegoats to bear the accumulated violence into death. We kill others to rescue ourselves from death. While it is true that the wages of sin is death and since all have sinned all will die (Rom 3:23; 6:23), the death which Scripture is most con-cerned with is not our own death, but the death of others by our own hand.

In human history, we have been able to justify the death of the other by blaming them for everything that has gone wrong (scapegoating), and by justifying the death of one as necessary for the good of all (sacrificing). We justify these scapegoating sacrifices by making the scapegoat into a monster. We convince ourselves that the other person must die because they are the evil sinner, the bringer of pain, sickness, and injustice, the creator of division and strife. In this way, we are able to hide the injustice of our own violence by claiming that our violence is justice.

But when Jesus died on the cross, it was evident to all that He was innocent of any wrongdoing. Though we tried to make Him a scapegoat by charging Him with blasphemy, the accusations brought against Him would not stick. When God raised Jesus from the dead, this was the divine vindication of Jesus, proving that all accusations brought against Jesus had been patently false.

So through His willing death as a truly innocent victim, Jesus unveiled the human reliance upon the death of the other as a means to achieve temporary peace. Though we can often rationally justify our violence against others, there is no way to rationally justify the murder of Jesus. But Jesus died willingly to reveal to us that just as we unjustly killed Him, so also, we have unjustly killed every victim in human history and that such violence in God's name must stop. "Jesus dies, not as a sacrifice, but in order that there may be no more sacrifices."[5]

---

[5] René Girard, *Things Hidden Since the Foundation of the World*, trans., Stephen Bann and Michael Metteer (Stanford, CA: Stanford University Press, 1987), 210.

To put it another way, "The gospel … is not ultimately about the exchange of victims, but about the ending of bloodshed."[6]

The cross reveals that the human desire to kill others in the name of justice (and in the name of God) as Jesus was killed, is not a divine characteristic, but human. God does not desire that anyone die for their sin, nor does He desire that anyone die for the sins of others, least of all His own Son! The death of Jesus on the cross at the hands of murderous religion revealed the truth about the death of the other once and for all. When we kill others in the name of God, we do so, not because God wanted them dead, but because we did. God is not the offended one; we are. When we kill others, we justify it in our own minds by saying that this person who must die has sinned and has so greatly offended God, that God wants them dead. But God does not want them dead. We want them dead, and we blame our murderous rage on God.

At the heart of every human lies a murderous desire, a desire to be like Cain and murder our brother. Even if we do not go as far as Cain in murdering our brother, we all have the desire of Abel's blood, which cries out from the ground for revenge. We say that such revenge is godly and divine, but really, it is our own heart crying out for revenge, and we place the blame for this desire for bloody revenge upon God. When we cry out for the death of the other in the name of God, we are seeking "to satisfy, not God, but our own need to avenge *on behalf of God,* a need projected as God's own need when it is ours."[7]

---

[6] S. Mark Heim, "Christ's Death to End Sacrifice." http://www.religion-online.org/showarticle.asp?title=2141 Last Accessed January 9, 2014.

[7] Walter Wink, *The Human Being: Jesus and the Enigma of the Son of Man* (Minneapolis: Fortress, 2002), 17.

This is how Jesus defeated death. As Jesus hung on the cross, He revealed to us not only the heart of God, but also the heart of man. He revealed the heart of God by crying out "Father, forgive them, for they know not what they do!" (Luke 23:34). He revealed that God's way to peace is not by killing others, but by forgiving others. He revealed that the only proper response to murder is forgiveness, for without forgiveness, murder leads to a cycle of violence that ends only in annihilation.

Jesus also revealed the heart of man. When we murdered Jesus as an innocent victim, and we murdered Him in the name of God, Jesus revealed what is in the heart of man. We kill others for our own benefit by making them out to be sinners and blasphemers so that we can kill them in God's name. Jesus defeats this murderous intent by showing us a different way. While the blood of Abel and all murdered victims after him cry out from the ground for vengeance, the blood of Jesus from the cross cried out for forgiveness. In this way, the blood of Jesus spoke a better word than the blood of Abel (Heb 12:24).

The word of forgiveness which Jesus spoke from the cross showed humanity once and for all that God was not angry with us for our sin, but had forgiven us. God even forgave the worst of all possible sins, the sin of killing God. The word of forgiveness spoken from the cross revealed that we do not achieve peace with God or with one another by killing others, but by forgiving others. Offering forgiveness in the midst of His death at the hands of others revealed the emptiness of the power of the death of others as a means of accomplishing peace. True and lasting peace comes only by unconditional forgiveness, which is what God has been extending to the world since the very beginning. By dying as He did, as a victim who was killed in the name of God, Jesus revealed what humans have always been doing when we kill others in God's name, and in this way, Jesus defeated the power of death. In this way, He also defeated the devil.

VICTORY OVER THE DEVIL

The victory of Jesus on the cross not only exposed the lie of sin and emptied death of its power, but also allowed Jesus to be victorious over the devil. We must not think however, that between His trial and His resurrection, Jesus engaged in some sort of cosmic Western gun duel with Satan. It was not as if Jesus and Satan met on some dusty road in hell, each one squinting and grimacing at the other waiting to see who would draw first with the end result being Satan flat on his back in the dust, saying, "Wow, that was fast!" No, that is not what happened at all.

To understand how Jesus was victorious over Satan on the cross, we must first understand that Satan is an accuser. In fact, "Satan" means "accuser." Satan's accusations are in two directions. First, Satan accuses mankind of wrongdoing before God, and second, Satan accuses God of wrongdoing before mankind. We see this, for example, in Job 1 where Satan accuses God of showing favoritism to Job, and in Revelation 12:9-11, where Satan is called the accuser of the brethren. Even in the very first temptation in Scripture, the serpent accuses God of withholding blessings from Adam and Eve. In speaking to Eve, Satan awakens her desire to be like God by implying that God is reserving a certain kind of knowledge only for Himself (Gen 3:1-5). These sorts of accusations are based on the lies of sin, and such accusations lead us to kill others in the name of God. Later, after they had sinned, Adam and Eve learn the blame game, so that Eve accuses the serpent, while Adam accuses Eve (and implies that God is really the one to blame).

This sort of pattern continues all the way throughout Scripture. Whenever Satan appears, he is accusing God or humans of something, and whenever humans lash out against others in violence it is because they first accused those others of wrongdoing. Frequently in Scripture, people also blame God for what goes wrong in this world. The tendency to accuse is closely related to the lies of sin and the desire to kill others in the name of God.

But this impulse to kill others in God's name is not from God, but from Satan. It is the spirit of the accuser that tempts us to condemn, judge, and accuse others of wrongdoing that makes them worthy of death. But in dying as a clearly innocent person, Jesus exposed the spirit of accusation that is within us all, and showed us that we do not know how to judge rightly and so should leave all judgment up to God. When religion and government wrongly accuses Jesus in the Gospels, we come face to face with the sad reality that we almost always wrongly accuse others when we call for their punishment and death.

This was the great problem with the Tree of the Knowledge of Good and Evil. There was not actually anything wrong with the knowledge that came by eating from this tree. The knowledge of good and evil is a knowledge that God Himself has. The reason, however, that God forbade Adam and Eve to eat of this tree and gain this knowledge is because humans lack something that God Himself has. We do not have omniscience. We do not know everything. The knowledge of good and evil is the knowledge of deciding between good and evil, right and wrong. This knowledge can only be correctly wielded by a being who knows all things. If all the facts are not known and all the circumstances are not understood, it is impossible to judge correctly between right and wrong, good and evil. Only God, who knows all, is able to make right judgments. And interestingly, God, who alone knows all, freely forgives all. This proves the truth of the statement that "To know all is to forgive all."

Eating from the Tree of the Knowledge of Good and Evil caused humans to try to make judgments between good and evil. But since we do not know all, we make bad judgments. We make accusations. We follow in the spirit of the accuser by blaming others for our sin, blaming God for what He has done, and killing others in God's name when things don't go as we planned. The spirit of accusation is the Satanic spirit. It is this accusatory spirit that Jesus exposed, and that Jesus invited us to cease using. Jesus called us to stop accusing others and leave all judgment up to God. Of course, God, who alone can make right judgments because He alone knows all things, chooses not to punish, accuse, and condemn, but instead to freely forgive, love, and restore.

It is Satan, therefore, not God, who demands punishment for sin. It is Satan, not God, who says that there must be a penalty for rebellion. It is Satan, not God, who condemns, accuses, and calls for vengeance. On the cross, Jesus revealed the truth about God's loving and limitless forgiveness, and so exposed the accusations of Satan as having nothing to do with God. The resurrection of Jesus proved that God did not support the death of Jesus and had nothing to do with it.

In this way, the resurrection blew the lid off the great scheme of Satan. From the very beginning, Satan has always used the name of God to carry out his own work. All the accusations and condemnations of the devil are done in God's name, under the guise of sacred religion. Satan "casts out Satan" in the name of God through the practices of religious accusations and sacrificial violence. In so doing, Satan only strengthens his power and expands his kingdom in this world. Whenever one person condemns and kills someone else in the name of God and for the sake of righteousness, this is really the power of Satan at work. And since the killing of a victim does seem to bring peace to warring factions, it is often assumed that God was behind the sacrifice and desired it, even though He did not.

But after Satan tried to do this very thing to Jesus, Jesus came back from the grave to reveal how wrong it all was. No victim in history had ever returned from the grave, but Jesus did. And normally, while a returning victim would cry out for revenge and retaliation, Jesus continued to teach only forgiveness, love, grace, and mercy. In this way, the accusatory lies of Satan were exposed and defeated. Satan had always depended on the human need to accuse and kill in God's name as the basis for his power. But when Jesus was raised from the dead, He revealed to the world that accusing and killing others in the name of God was never God's desire or intention, but was instead the desire and intention of Satan instead. In Jesus we saw that God was not the one calling for the death of our enemies, but it was we who wanted to kill our enemies, and we accused them and killed them in God's name to justify and hide from our own evil actions.

Throughout all of human history, Satan has pulled the wool over human eyes, and made us to believe that God was on our side and against our enemies. But on the cross and through the resurrection, this entire perspective and scheme was exposed as having nothing whatsoever to do with God. The cross of Jesus is a "divine trap, a ruse of God that is even stronger and cleverer than Satan's ruses."[8]

> [In killing Jesus], Satan believed he was protecting his kingdom, defending his possessions, not realizing that, in fact, he was doing the very opposite. He did exactly as God had forseen. Only Satan could have set in motion the process of his own destruction without suspecting anything was wrong. ... [Yet] The trick that traps Satan does not include the least bit of either violence or dishonesty on God's part. It is not really a ruse or a trick; it is rather the inability of the prince of the world to understand the divine love. ... God does not act treacherously, even toward Satan, but allows himself to be crucified for the salvation of humankind, something beyond Satan's conception.[9]

The early church called this the *Risus Paschalis,* the Easter Laugh. After the Easter celebration, the people would tell jokes to one another, "to commemorate the divine joke, played on the devil, of the resurrection of Jesus."[10] By killing Jesus, Satan "overstepped all bounds, overreaching any authority he may have had by killing someone not legitimately subject to death. By doing so, he forfeited his rule."[11] In killing Jesus as a scapegoat, Satan killed the only person in history who could clearly demonstrate that He had done nothing worthy of condemnation and killing, and in so doing, he emptied his kingdom of its power. The resurrection of Jesus caused Satan to tip

---

[8] René Girard, *I See Satan Fall Like Lightning* (Maryknoll, NY: Orbis, 1999), 148.

[9] Ibid., 151-152.

[10] Nathan Rieger in Brad Jersak and Michael Hardin, eds., *Stricken by God? Nonviolent Identification and the Victory of Christ* (Grand Rapids: Eerdmans, 2007), 379.

[11] Ibid., 381.

his hand, and we saw that he was only bluffing. The power of Satan to accuse and condemn in God's name was revealed to be nothing more than a lie which we told ourselves to make us feel better about what we were doing to others.

In the wisdom of God, the trap set by Satan was the mechanism by which Satan and the powers of violence were defeated. The accusatory and legalistic requirements of Satan were the exact means by which God exposed the emptiness of Satan's power. In Jesus Christ, God nailed the power of accusation and scapegoating to the cross, and subjected them to public humiliation, exposing them for what they truly were, as nothing more than lies of the devil (Col 2:14-15; cf. 1 Cor 2:8). As a result, we must stop all judgment and condemnation of others (Col 2:16), choosing only to love and forgive others as God has loved and forgiven us.

So it is not God, but Satan, who demands punishment for our crimes. It is not God, but Satan, who demands death and blood as payment for sin. This is why Jesus said that Satan was a liar and a murderer from the beginning (John 8:44). The main lie of sin is that God is angry at us because of our sin, and that we must do something to appease the wrath of God. We also saw that the main belief about death is that the death of someone else is required to achieve our own safety and security.

We are now seeing that Satan, the accuser, is behind both of these lies. Satan lies to us, telling us that God is angry at us because of our sin, and that God requires us to repay Him somehow for the sin we have committed. Satan also lies to us about violence being the only real solution to violence. "Kill or be killed," Satan whispers. "Strike first; strike hard." We are told that it is better for one to die than for thousands to suffer, and so must kill the one, even if that one is innocent. And when we use scapegoating violence, we become convinced that the problem is not in us, but in the other person. It is *they* who are guilty, not us, and so it is *they* who must die.

On the cross, Jesus exposed all these lies for what they are, and in so doing, was victorious over the devil by exposing his accusations for the lies that they are. The death of Jesus revealed that God is not angry about sin, but instead loves all people infinitely and extends forgiveness freely to all people unconditionally. On the cross, Jesus revealed that this forgiveness God extends to us is the only way to achieve peace and safety in our life. Jesus also revealed that if violence leads to death (because there is sin in this world), it is better to submit ourselves to death than to seek the death of the other, for seeking to kill the other results only in a rapid escalation of violence that will threaten to kill and destroy all.

Through His death and resurrection, Jesus was victorious over the lies and deceits of the devil that had captivated and victimized all of humanity since the very beginning. Jesus exposed these lies as having nothing whatsoever to do with God, and in so doing, called us to withhold all judgments and suspend all accusations so that we too, like God, can extend love, grace, mercy, and forgiveness to all.

THE DEATH OF NON-VIOLENCE

In this discussion of the Non-Violent view of the atonement, we have seen that Jesus was victorious over sin, death, and the devil. We have seen that through His victory over these three forces in the world, Jesus revealed that God was supremely non-violent and that God always loves, always forgives, and always seeks fellowship and relationship with us. All the ideas about God's anger toward us, the requirement to repay a debt of sin, the necessity of God to punish sin, and the demand to condemn those who do sin, are nothing more than lies.

These lies that Jesus exposed through the crucifixion and resurrection not only reveal that we are victims to these lies, but also that we are the victimizers. We use these lies that have victimized us to victimize others. God wants all this victimization to stop, which is why He exposed these lies for what they were through the person and work of Jesus Christ. The lies that Jesus exposed do not only reveal the loving and forgiving heart of God, but also reveal the murderous and violent heart of man. Once we see the reality, the revelation of Jesus calls us to live differently. We too can live non-violently, seeking to love and forgive others rather than condemn, accuse, or kill them in God's name. Obviously, such ideas are not very popular among many people. We naturally want to exert our rights, defend our privileges, and condemn or kill any who get in our way.

It is partly for this reason that Non-Violent views of the atonement fell out of favor in some forms of Christianity and why Non-Violent views are often rejected today. Let us look briefly at how and why *Christus Victor* and other Non-Violent views of the atonement ceased being the common view of the atonement in Western Christianity.

Remember, first of all, that Non-Violent views of the atonement were the *only* views within Christianity for about the first 300 years of our history. Alternative views did not become prominent or popular until much later in Christian history, and it was not really until the Middle Ages after Anselm developed an early form of the Penal Substitutionary view that Non-Violent views became less prominent. This development was discussed above in the section about Penal Substitution. This doesn't mean that Non-Violent views disappeared completely. During the Reformation, for example, Martin Luther attempted to revive and return to a Non-Violent view of the atonement and nearly everything he wrote and taught was centered on this perspective. Nevertheless, his followers failed to maintain Luther's view of the atonement and returned to the Penal Substitution view, which has been the dominant view in Western Christianity ever since. Eastern Christianity, however, has always held a Non-Violent view, even to this day.[12]

So if Non-Violent views of the atonement were the original views within Christianity, what happened? Why and how did they lose prominence within Christian theology?

The primary reason that Non-Violent views of the atonement fell out of favor is "not because of intrinsic inadequacies, but because it was subversive to the church's role as state religion."[13] The process of decline began when the church gained the power of the sword under Emperor Constantine in the 4th Century. During the reign of Constantine, Christianity became the official religion of the Roman Empire, and he used the power of politics, the lure of money, and the strength of the military to extend the reach and influence of Christianity within the Roman Empire. Not surprisingly, when an Emperor and his state-sanctioned theologians seek to defend their use of money, power, and military might to advance the cause of Christianity, the idea that Jesus was against the use of such things becomes increasingly unpopular. Non-violent views of the atonement

---

[12] For a historical summary of the Christus Victor view in church tradition, see Gustaf Aulén, *Christus Victor: An Historical Study of the Three Main Types of the Idea of the Atonement* (Eugene, OR: Wipf & Stock, 1931).. Chapters 2-6 of Aulen's book show how the early church almost universally held to a Non-Violent atonement, and how this view of the atonement was the dominant view up until the Reformation.

[13] Walter Wink, *The Powers that Be: Theology for a New Millennium* (New York: Galilee, 1998), 90.

fell out of favor as Christianity embraced violent methods of accumulating power, wealth, and influence.

When the church works along with the government to rule, the church has great difficulty in disagreeing with the government about how to rule within this world. Under Constantine and during the centuries that followed, the church could no longer say that Jesus rejected military might, the glory of wealth, or the power over other people, for this would endanger the church's position and prominence within the government of the Western world. When the government looks to the church for blessings on wars and expansion efforts, the church cannot safely teach that God is essentially non-violent and is not opposed to your enemies the way you are. So the church chose to keep their wealth and influence rather than stand up for non-violence and risk losing the position and power they had gained. This was not an intentional departure from the teachings of Jesus as much as it was pragmatic. The church truly thought that they could harness and control the worldly powers of money, position, and influence.

As the church abandoned its calling to critique and challenge the governments of this world, the message of the gospel began to increasingly focus on the transaction of individualistic salvation between God and man instead of God's call for all people, tongues, tribes, and nations to fall under the Lordship of the non-violent Jesus Christ. Rather than focusing on Jesus' life and ministry as the keys to transform and redeem society, the church began to teach that the purpose of Christ's coming was only to transform and redeem individuals within this world while we wait to go to heaven after we die.

The church no longer saw the demonic as lodged in the empire, but in the empire's enemies. Atonement became a highly individual transaction between the believer and God; society was as-sumed to be Christian, so the idea that the work of Christ entails the radical critique of society was largely abandoned.[14]

Eventually, Non-Violent views of the atonement became a mi-nority position within the Western church. For the past 300 years, relatively few people have even known that there is such a thing as a Non-Violent view of the atonement.

But the church's awareness of the teachings and message of Jesus is changing once again.

THE RESURRECTION OF NON-VIOLENCE

Just as an embrace of political power and influence led to the church abandoning Non-Violent views of the atonement, so also, wherever Christians start to turn away from the tempta-tions of power, money, and control, Non-Violent views of the atonement are rapidly accepted and taught. Since Non-Violent views of the atonement were rejected in tandem with the church abandoning its critique of society and empire, it is no accident that whenever and wherever Christians take up the critique of society and empire, Non-Violent views of the atonement theology come back into prominence. Once people begin to see that the principles and values of the Kingdom of God stand opposed to many of the values and principles of the governments of men and the surrounding society, Non-Violent views become the preferred explanation for what God has done in Jesus Christ to overturn and defeat the domination system

---

[14] Walter Wink, *Engaging the Powers: Discernment and Resistance in a World of Domination* (Minneapolis: Fortress, 1992), 150.

found within society and culture. It is this sort of resurrection of Non-Violent views of the atonement that Western Christianity is experiencing today.

While Non-Violent views of the atonement were the primary (and maybe the sole) atonement views of the early church, they are also the primary position among Christians who see that the gospel message contains not just information that individuals must believe in order to go to heaven when they die, but also (mostly) a radical announcement about the way this world has gone wrong and what God has done in Jesus Christ to restore righteousness, love, peace, and justice to this world. Whenever and wherever the gospel message is appreciated in its entirety as a message that contains truths not just for the afterlife but for this life as well, Non-Violent views of the atonement are taught and proclaimed as the foundation for that gospel message. It was this way in the early church, and it is this way now among those who follow their example of calling society and empire to a different way of living within the Kingdom of God on earth.

One of the other reasons that Non-Violent views of the atonement are making a comeback is because more and more people are beginning to see that such views incorporate and include most of the strengths of the other theories of the atonement while avoiding many of their weaknesses. For example, the Bible is filled with references to Jesus dying in our place and bearing the penalty for sin that was due to fall upon us (cf. Isa 53:4-5; Rom 3:23-25; 2 Cor 5:21; Heb 2:17; 9:26; 1 John 2:2). The frequency of such substitutionary language is one of the great supporting factors to the Penal Substitution view of the atonement.

Non-Violent views, however, can also affirm the substitutionary death of Jesus on the cross for humanity. Since, in Non-

Violent views, all of humanity is a victim to the lies about sin, God, and justice, Jesus entered into the role of victim so that He might become one of us and also expose to us our tendency to accuse and blame innocent victims. Jesus substituted Himself for every victim, to show us that He is with us when we are victims and also to show us the illegitimacy of victimizing others. Yet in contrast to Penal Substitution, a Non-Violent view is able to say that Jesus died in our place, not to satisfy the demands of an angry God, but rather to reveal God's complete love and solidarity with mankind by allowing the full outpouring of wrath from sin, death, and the devil to fall upon His back instead of upon ours. In this way, we still get the substitutionary offering of Jesus—which is the strength of Penal Substitution—but are able to avoid the objectionable idea that the wrath which came upon Jesus was from God (See Appendix 1 for a discussion of the wrath of God). While Jesus was our "substitute," He did not die to satisfy God's wrath. His death was not *penal*, that is, there was no punishment involved. God was not angry. God was not demanding blood. God was not withholding forgiveness until He got paid for sin. A Non-Violent view of the atonement embraces the strengths of Penal Substitution while avoiding its weaknesses.

The same is true of the Ransom to Satan view. While Scripture does seem to indicate that Satan made some demands of God and of humanity for the sin we committed, we must not fall into the trap of thinking that Jesus paid a ransom price to Satan for humanity. In the Ransom to Satan view, Satan appears to be a cosmic terrorist who holds humanity captive until the ransom price is paid. But God does not negotiate with terrorists. (He doesn't nuke them either.) The Non-Violent view of the atonement can affirm, along with the Ransom to Satan view, that humanity was held captive by Satan and that Jesus set us free. When Jesus came, and especially when He died on the cross, He did not pay off the devil, but defeated the devil once and for all. The life, ministry, death, and resurrection of Jesus were a rescue operation, not a secret payoff transaction between God and the devil.

It is for these sorts of reasons that the Non-Violent view is making a bit of a comeback today. One main objection to the Non-Violent view, however, is that simply by looking around at life, it does not appear that Jesus was victorious over sin, death and the devil. As people look around at the world and see that sin, death, and evil occur everywhere all the time. But it is important to recognize that we live in an interim period between the time when the walls of our prison have come down and when the rule and reign of God comes fully to bear. The victory has been won, but all the prisoners have not yet been let out of their chains.

This is why gospel proclamation is so important. The gospel announcement is not a message about how people can go to heaven after they die, but is about how God in Jesus has demolished the prison gates, has jailed the jailor, and is now coming, hallway by hallway, cell by cell, to set the captives free (cf. Luke 4:18-19). Furthermore, those of us who have been set free are not called to leave the prison, but to go further in to bring hope and healing to those who have not yet heard. We are called to follow Jesus in proclaiming the arrival of the reign of God and His promise of peace and rest. Jesus has not broken the gates of hell and imprisoned the jailor just to knock down the prison walls, but rather to turn this prison into paradise, and to resurrect the garden upon which these prison walls were built. This is the gospel message and this is the gospel that the Non-Violent view proclaims.

As can be seen, the Non-Violent view of the atonement is not just a way of understanding what Jesus did on the cross. It also has far reaching ramifications for all areas of life and theology. As much as the Non-Violent view transforms and reshapes our understanding of what Jesus accomplished through His death and resurrection, its implications do not stop there. The Non-Violent view is more than just a way of viewing the atonement. When the Non-Violent view of the atonement is adopted, it cascades down into all other areas of life and theology, affecting not just how we live as followers of Jesus in this world, but also how we view God, Scripture, mankind, sin, politics, religion, and culture. It is to these subjects we now turn.

PART II:

THE NON-VIOLENT ATONEMENT AND THEOLOGY

Most of theology is like an Excel spreadsheet. In a spreadsheet where the various cells are all dependent upon the data entered into other cells, when you change the data in one cell it has a cascading effect on the information found in numerous other cells. This is why corporations sometimes have mistakes in their accounting reports. If a single number is entered incorrectly, or if a decimal point is out of place, it can have a ripple effect throughout the rest of the spreadsheet, and ultimately to the financial reports of the business.

This is true for theology as well. If someone slightly changes their view of Ecclesiology or Eschatology, such changes will often have ripple effects throughout the rest of their theology, some of which may not be discerned for many years. So, for example, if someone changes their view on the rapture of the church, this will have ramifications for how that person views the passages in Scripture which are often used to teach the rapture of the church, which will, in turn, have ramifications on how the Bible is read and interpreted as well as the role and function of the church in society and culture. These changes will affect how we view the purpose of humanity in this world, the effects of sin, and what we believe God is doing with mankind regarding sin. The changes will continue to ripple on from there. So, one change in Eschatology creates further changes in Bibliology, Ecclesiology, Anthropology, Hamartiology, and Theology Proper. These secondary changes create more changes later on.

If this is what happens when we change our view on something like the rapture, we should expect even greater changes when we alter our view of the atonement. Since the crucifixion and resurrection of Jesus are at the center of Christian theology, a change in how one views the atonement will create massive upheavals in every other area of theology as well. A change in how we view what Jesus did on the cross will not only change how we view the rest of Jesus' life (Christology), but also how we view God (Theology Proper), Scripture (Bibliology), humanity (Anthropology), sin (Hamartiology), forgiveness and salvation (Soteriology), human history and culture (Sociology), how we are to live as members of God's family in this world (Ecclesiology), and God's ultimate goal for humanity (Eschatology).

As my own view on the atonement has changed over the years, I have experienced many of these theological shifts in my own thinking. Some of the major changes brought about by the Non-Violent view of the atonement will be discussed in the ten short chapters below. Each of these ten chapters requires a whole book to explain in more detail, but I present them here simply for the sake of introducing some of the changes that may occur to your theology if you adopt a Non-Violent view of the atonement. These changes do not necessarily occur in *all* theologians who adopt a Non-Violent view of the atonement, nor are they necessarily changes you *must* adopt in your theology if you accept a Non-Violent atonement. I raise these issues only to show how my own theology has changed and also to indicate how your theology also might change if you adopt a Non-Violent view of the atonement.

CHAPTER 3

BRINGS CONTINUITY
TO THE LIFE OF JESUS

A Non-Violent atonement helps bring continuity to the entire life of Jesus. This is because a Non-Violent view of the atonement concerns not just what happened to Jesus while He hung on the cross, or what happened to Him during the three days between His death and resurrection, but relates to everything Jesus said and did during His three years of ministry. While other atonement theology primarily focuses on the cross, the Non-Violent atonement brings continuity to the entire life of Jesus, with the crucifixion and resurrection as the pinnacle and crowning achievement of all that He lived and taught. His life was a revelation of the reign of God, His death a revelation of the love of God, and His resurrection a revelation of the victory of God. In other atonement theologies, the only thing that *really* matters in Jesus' life is the final hours on the cross and the resurrection that follows; everything else is just prelude. But in Non-Violent theology, *everything* Jesus did in His life was for the purpose of introducing the world to the reign of God and inaugurating the Kingdom of God, which He did by defeating sin, death, and the devil, not just by His life but also by His death. Therefore, the Non-Violent view of the atonement allows everything in the life of Jesus to be of utmost importance, not just the last few hours on the cross. His crowning victory, of course, was on the cross, and it is there that His ultimate victory was accomplished, but all of Jesus' teachings, miracles, and actions throughout all of His life served as preliminary battles to rescue people from what holds them captive.

A Non-Violent atonement even sheds new light on the events and circumstances surrounding the birth of Jesus. His birth reveals that a new way of living and a new value system had dawned upon mankind. Since Jesus was born in a stable to a woman who became pregnant out of wedlock, and was welcomed by foreigners and shepherds, the birth of Jesus indicated that the life and love of God was available to all and was for all, regardless of status, gender, or race.

Furthermore, the teachings and parables of Jesus were intended to announce the arrival of the Kingdom of God and to reveal that God was not angry with humanity but was full of love, grace, mercy, and forgiveness. The miracles and parables of Jesus further revealed the emptiness of religion as a means of approaching God. Jesus announced that people no longer needed holy places such as temples, holy people such as priests, or holy procedures such as sacrifices and rituals to approach God. Instead, anybody and everybody could approach God directly through Jesus Christ.

In this way, everything that Jesus did, said, and taught during His three years of ministry was designed to show that He was victorious over sin, death, and the devil. He forgave sins without forcing people to go through the religious sacrificial system. He healed people of their infirmities, which were often associated with their iniquity. He hung out with sinners, tax-collectors, and prostitutes, showing that there was no chasm between God and sinful humanity. He cast out demons, showing that Satan and his minions had no power over Jesus or in His Kingdom. He even raised people from the dead, showing that in Him, death itself was defeated.

The Non-Violent view of the atonement introduces continuity to the life of Jesus Christ. If the primary purpose for the coming of Jesus was to die for the sins of the world, then there would have been no real reason for him to teach others and perform the miracles that He did. Instead, He could have just shown up one day and said, "Okay, I'm here! Now let me die!" In the other atonement theories, while Jesus lived His life as a human to accomplish a variety of things, none of these really had anything to do with His ultimate victory which He won through dying on the cross. According to these other theories, Jesus came to teach us about God, or to raise the bar of morality over that of Moses to prove that we are all sinners in the hands of an angry God, or to simply prove how righteous and powerful He was, but none of this matters much for the atonement theory itself. Not so with the Non-Violent atonement! Everything Jesus said and did, from His conception to His resurrection, lends support to the truth that Jesus came to set the captives free by defeating sin, death, and the devil.

Therefore, a Non-Violent atonement alone allows the life and ministry of Jesus to be more than just a long introduction to the crucifixion. The Non-Violent view of the atonement brings continuity to the entire life of Jesus, showing that everything Jesus said and did leading up to the crucifixion was part and parcel with the crucifixion and resurrection of Jesus.

CHAPTER 4

REVEALS THE TRUTH ABOUT GOD

The Non-Violent view of the atonement also changes how we view God. J. Denny Weaver argues that our atonement theology and our view of God are intimately connected.

> Ultimately, atonement theology is actually a discussion of our image of God—one who defeats violence with superior violence and reconciles sin on the basis of a violent death, or a God who triumphs over evil and reconciles sinners nonviolently through resurrection.[1]

The other atonement perspectives, especially the Penal Substitution view, portray God as somewhat schizophrenic regarding how He feels about mankind. On the one hand He loves us and wants to spend eternity with us, but on the other hand He hates us and wants to send us all to hell. This perspective about God is partly because the other atonement views take a chronological approach to building their theology of God. They begin in

---

[1] J. Denny Weaver in Brad Jersak and Michael Hardin, eds., *Stricken by God? Nonviolent Identification and the Victory of Christ* (Grand Rapids: Eerdmans, 2007), 340.

Genesis and work their way through the Bible to learn about God and what He is like. When they do this, they get an impression from many Old Testament texts that God is angry with sinners and wants only to drown, burn, kill, or slaughter all those who do not obey Him (see Genesis through Judges). But then Jesus comes along, and takes all this divine anger upon Himself (see the Gospels). In these other views, even though Jesus bore the brunt of God's wrath, God is still angry at humanity even today so that eventually Jesus comes around to God's way of viewing the world and shows up at the end of time to cut down His enemies and incinerate His foes (see Revelation).

The Non-Violent view of the atonement approaches Scripture and theological development from a different perspective. Rather than developing theology by reading the Bible chronologically, Non-Violent theology reads the Bible *Christologically*. In other words, rather than beginning with Genesis and working our way through the Bible to see what we can learn about God, a Non-Violent approach to God begins with Jesus Christ, and then reads the Bible and seeks to understand God in light of what we see in Jesus. This seems to be what Jesus Himself taught us to do (see John 14:9; Luke 24:44-45), and what Paul and the apostles seemed to have done as well in basing their theology on what they saw in Jesus Christ (cf. Col 1:15; Heb 1:3).

More specifically still, to see what God is like, a Non-Violent theology begins not just with Jesus, but primarily with what we see in Jesus as He dies on the cross. Paul resolved to know nothing but Christ and Him crucified as he went about planting churches and spreading the gospel (1 Cor 2:2). He did this because it is on the cross that Jesus most fully reveals God to us. This is why many Non-Violent proponents often refer to "cruciform" theology, or what I refer to as "crucivision" theology. We cannot begin to understand God until we view God through the cross of Jesus Christ. If we want to understand what God is like, we must have a crucivision of God by viewing God through the crucifixion of Jesus.

When we view God as being fully revealed in Jesus, and especially in Jesus as He died on the cross, what sort of crucivision of God do we see? We do not see an angry God who is out to kill, maim, drown, or burn humanity in hell. Instead, we see a God who is willing to be maimed, tortured, and killed *for* us and *by* us, rather than do such things *to* us.

This is completely contrary to the way many people, including many Christians, view God. When people have an angry view of God which is developed by beginning with an Old Testament perspective of God, they see the crucifixion of Jesus as a horror. When people have an angry view of God, they see God as being so upset about sin that He just has to take out His anger on someone, and Jesus is the poor wretch upon whom the wrath of God falls. Such an idea is terrifying. People realize that if God is willing to brutalize His only Son to satisfy His anger toward humanity, then God is also willing to do similar things to us.

But if we begin with Jesus on the cross, and recognize that God is fully revealing Himself in Jesus as He dies on the cross, then an entirely different picture emerges. We see that God is not seeking to vent His anger out on somebody, but instead entered into our world so that we might vent our anger out upon Him. When we begin with Jesus, we see that God is not sitting up in heaven with His arms folded across His chest and a scowl on His face waiting for us come to Him on our knees begging and pleading for His forgiveness. No, we see that He entered into our fallen world and did everything necessary to reconcile us to Himself (2 Cor 5:18-21). It was not God who needed to be reconciled to us, but we who needed to be reconciled to Him. Just like in the Garden of Eden, God did not separate or hide Himself from us; it is we who separated and hid ourselves from Him. Jesus didn't die to satisfy God. Jesus died to satisfy us. We thought He was angry at us, but He was not. We were angry at Him (for no real reason whatsoever), and so He came to us, loved us, and showed us that He forgave us. He even let us kill Him. And when He did not retaliate against us for the greatest crime in history, we saw once and for all how much He loved us.

Before Jesus showed us by dying on the cross what God is truly like, we were terrified of God and tried to keep our distance from God. Sin and shame separated us from God; not God from us. Our sin and shame caused us to see God as a fearful, terrifying Being, who hated us because of our rebellion and who only wanted to pour out His wrath and vengeance upon us. But this is not what God is like, and He wanted to show us what He is truly like, and so He came in the person of Jesus Christ, and died on the cross. Why? To take the thing that was separating us from Him, and take it onto Himself. But it did not consume Him; He consumed it.

> The cross exposes the lie of our misconstrued images of God. Instead of a distant accusing figure all too willing to use his awesome power to punish human error, in Jesus God reveals himself to be accepting and forgiving, a God whose ultimate solution is not to destroy through awesome power, but to heal and restore by shouldering suffering that is not rightly his.[2]

---

[2] Mark D. Baker in ibid., 299.

On the cross, God showed us what He is really like. He showed us who He really is. He showed us that He loves us, forgives us, and wants to have a relationship with us. Jesus did not go to the cross so that God could love us once again. No, Jesus went to the cross to show us that God has always loved us. Jesus went to the cross to rescue us from our sin and shame so that He could invite us into the loving relationship with God that He has always wanted.

It is on the cross where God is most fully revealed in Jesus. And it is there that God revealed how He has always been dying for us, crucifying His holiness and His character on the cross of our sin. Jesus revealed God to us by entering into our world and letting us blame Him for all that has gone wrong in this world.

> God is not a stern and inflexible magistrate but a loving Abba. Why then was a redemptive act necessary? Because our resentment toward God and our will to kill leaves us unable to turn to God. "God needs no reparation, but human beings must be extracted from their own prison if they are to be capable of accepting the pure gift of freely offered love. ... It is not God who must be appeased, but humans who must be delivered from their hatred" of God.[3]

> Dare we discern anything so outrageous as the idea that here God is making an atonement towards man for all that his desired creation costs man in the making: that he was making love's amends to all those who feel, and have felt, that they cannot forgive God for all the pains which life has foisted, unwanted, upon them? It

---

[3] Walter Wink, *Engaging the Powers: Discernment and Resistance in a World of Domination* (Minneapolis: Fortress, 1992), 150. His quote is from Raymund Schwager, *Must There Be Scapegoats? Violence and Redemption in the Bible* (New York: Crossroad, 2000), 209.

is certainly true that man, struggling to perceive the justice which his God-like nature demands, cannot forgive God for the fate which freedom's caprice has brought his way.

Love in God's fashion is indeed outrageous and a scandal because it does stoop and condescend to what, by lesser standards, it need not. Perhaps God in his love stands, not only as the bestower of forgiveness, but as the Father who, for the sake of the created whose glory is his desire, even stoops to invite the forgiveness he cannot deserve in order to make it one degree easier for man to be drawn into the orbit of love ...[4]

In our hearts, at our most honest moments, we all feel that God has wronged us, that He is not doing a good job of running this world, and that as long as heads are rolling, His too must roll, and God, in His outrageous, shocking, scandalous, shameful love, agrees! The pain and suffering of this world was the price for the freedom of love which He wants to share with us. But as we develop and grow into this freedom, there is great suffering and pain. God, since He set up this world this way, takes responsibility for pain and the suffering. He becomes one of us, and takes our sin upon Himself so that He might be both the forgiver and the forgiven. In Jesus, God asks for our forgiveness so that we also, in Jesus, might both bestow and receive forgiveness. "Jesus did not come to change the mind of God about humanity. Jesus came to change the mind of humanity about God."[5]

The Non-Violent view of the atonement shows that God is not angry with humanity, nor is He full of wrath and venge-

---

[4] Andrew Elphinstone, *Freedom, Suffering and Love* (London: SCM Press, 1976), 147.

[5] Richard Rohr in Jersak and Hardin, eds., *Stricken by God?*, 209.

ance, inflicting pain and punishment upon the world the way we all think. Instead, God is grieved about our plunge into sin and is doing everything possible to alleviate the pain and protect us from the fallout of sin, even to the point of letting us blame Him for the sin and evil we ourselves commit. Out of His great love for us, God has always been forgiving us, not only for the sins we commit because we are sinners, but also (and especially) for the sins we commit in His name. God has never retaliated against us for our sin, or for the blame we pour upon Him for the sin we commit. He does not retaliate, nor does He demand payment for our grievances against Him. God is not angry with us over our sin, nor has He ever been angry.

Once we see this in Jesus on the cross, we read the Bible with new eyes, and begin to see that this foundational truth of Scripture is revealed on nearly every page. God looks like Jesus and because Jesus always loves and always forgives, this is what God has always been doing as well.

CHAPTER 5

REVEALS THE TRUTH ABOUT SCRIPTURE

The Non-Violent view of the atonement allows us to see God through the lens of Jesus on the cross, which in turn provides a whole new perspective on Scripture. When we read the Bible with crucivision eyes, the entire Bible becomes a brand new book. It becomes a book that reveals to us that we humans are the ones who cause bad things to happen in this world. It becomes a book that reveals God as only loving and forgiving. It shows us that when bad things happen in this world, it is not because God sent such things or even allowed them to happen, but that such things occur because of our own sin and because we live in a world with an infinite number of variables beyond our understanding or control. We also learn that God is not absent, neglectful, or inactive in our pain, but enters into it with us. God loves us so much, He even allows us to "crucify" His name by blaming Him for every evil action and bad event that occurs. Just as Jesus bore the sins of the world on Himself as a testimony of His love for us, so also, God has always been bearing the sin, blame, and shame of the sins of the world upon Himself out of His great love for us. When God looks guilty for the sins of the world, it is not because He *is* guilty, but because, just like Jesus, He has allowed us to lay our sin and guilt upon His shoulders.

What we see about God in Jesus Christ helps explain the way God is portrayed in the Old Testament. By being killed in the name of God, Jesus revealed that we have been sinning and murdering from the beginning in the name of God, and that every evil done in the name of God was not because God wanted or commanded these things done. Instead, we ourselves wanted to do such things but didn't want to take the blame or responsibility for them, and so we blamed God. Just as with the killing of Jesus in God's name, so also, we humans throughout history have killed, destroyed, and stolen from others in God's name. We put God's stamp of approval on our own evil actions, thereby making Him the scapegoat and relieving us of the guilt and shame we feel for our sin.

In this way, the Old Testament is not primarily a revelation from God about God, but rather a revelation from God about humanity. In many ways, the Old Testament does more to reveal ourselves to us than it does to reveal God to us. It reveals what is in the heart of humankind more than it reveals what is in the heart of God. It is true what James says: the Scriptures are a mirror by which we see our own face (Jas 1:23). Furthermore, we turn away from what we see about ourselves within the pages of Scripture to our own detriment. This helps solve the debate over inspiration and inerrancy. When we realize that the Bible is God's inspired and inerrant revelation to humanity about humanity and what is in the heart of humanity, we can easily understand why there is so much "wrong" being done within the pages of Scripture in the name of God.

> Though the problem of violence originates with humans, the response to it implicates both God and humanity. Caught up in a mimetic rivalry *they attribute to God*, humans then conceive God as the mirror image of their own escalating conflict. … If we are to judge from the Bible's own plot, none of these [violent] representations [of God] give a full or adequate characterization of God's true nature. But they do tell fundamental truths about the human condition and our relation with God.[1]

So, Scripture is not only a revelation of God to us; it is also a revelation of man to us. Both are revealed inerrantly within the pages of Scripture. How can we know when Scripture is revealing God to us and when it is revealing man to us? We can know it by looking at Jesus. He is the perfect and fullest revelation of God. So whenever a depiction of God in the Old Testament does not look like the depiction of Jesus in the Gospels, we can know that those Old Testament passages are not revealing God to us, but are instead revealing the heart of man, and how we project our sin and evil upon God in order to make ourselves feel better about what we are doing.

This is especially true when it comes to the violent portions of the Old Testament. As René Girard points out in his books, but especially in *Sacred Violence* and *The Scapegoat,* all human cultures and societies throughout time seek to bring peace between warring factions by turning the wrath of both groups upon an outside third party, and they nearly always do this in the name of God. They believe that by killing this outsider in the name of God, God will bring peace to their community. People believe that this newcomer or outsider is the one who

---

[1] S. Mark Heim, *Saved From Sacrifice: A Theology of the Cross* (Grand Rapids: Eerdmans, 2006), 73-74., italics mine.

has created all the problems in their culture and society, and so by killing this other person, they destroy the disruptor of peace, the bringer of sin, and the creator of chaos. Since God clearly wants peace and unity, it is obviously God's will that this outsider be killed. And usually, a temporary peace results from the death of this scapegoat.

This is what happened in the tinderbox of Jerusalem when the religious and political factions united together against Jesus. They sought to create peace by blaming Jesus for their problems and killing Him in the name of God. The death of Jesus was not something God wanted or demanded in order to forgive sins, but was something people wanted in order to restore order and bring peace to a situation that was escalating out of control (cf. Luke 23:12; John 11:50). When we see how the religious and political authorities collaborated to kill Jesus in God's name so that there might be peace to Jerusalem, we gain a clear revelation of what was going on in all violent Old Testament texts when people kill others in God's name to bring peace to their tribe or nation.

Jesus, of course, never behaved this way, which reveals to us that God never behaved this way either. When we see passages in the Old Testament that portray God as killing His enemies, what we actually have in those passages is an accurate and inerrant divine revelation about what is in the heart of mankind. The Bible is perfectly true, not because the Bible always presents a true reflection of God, but because the Bible is a perfect mirror into which we look to see the reflection of our own human hearts. The sections that are "wrong" about God are the sections that are perfectly accurate about us. Mark Heim explains:

What is violence doing in the Bible? It is telling us the truth, the truth about our human condition, about the fundamental dynamics that lead to human bloodshed, and most particularly, the truth about the integral connection between religion and violence. There is no way to be truthful without exhibiting these things. If we complain that the tales of Genesis and the bloody sacrifices of Leviticus, and the fire for revenge in the Psalms, are too sordidly, familiarly human to have any place in religious revelation, we make an interesting admission that they reveal our humanity all too well.

What is violence doing in the Bible? It is showing us the nature of the mimetic conflict that threatens to destroy human community. It is showing us the religious dynamic of scapegoating sacrifice that arises to allay such crisis. It is letting us hear the voices of the persecuted victims and their pleas for revenge and vindication. ... The Old Testament is an antimyth. It is thick with bodies, the voices of victims and threatened victims.[2]

The Bible is violent because humans are violent. We are uncomfortable with the violence in Scripture because it reveals the violence that is in the human heart. By blaming this violence upon God, we commit the same sin that our ancestors committed when they first engaged in their violent behavior. We must break out of the cycle of mimetic violence by admitting that these violent texts do not reveal God to us, but instead reveal our own violent hearts.

When we read in the Bible about God doing and saying things that look completely unlike Jesus dying on the cross, it is in those instances that we can understand that the Bible is showing us our own face rather than the face of God. It is in

---

[2] Ibid., 101, 103.

those instances where we need to carefully observe what the mirror of Scripture shows us, and then make sure that we do not turn away, forgetting what we have seen, but instead take steps to correct what we see in our own lives.

As long as we ignore the revelation of God in Jesus Christ on the cross, and deceive ourselves into thinking that the revelation about man in the Old Testament is really a revelation about God, we can continue to behave in sinful and selfish behaviors, all the while assuming that we are doing what God wants. But when we realize that God is like Jesus, and that the un-Christlike behavior of God in various Old Testament texts is actually an inspired revelation about how we humans do evil in the name of God, we can no longer continue to live as we were, but must take steps to live like Jesus while not blaming our evil upon God. All examples of violence in Scripture are not given to show us how to behave, but instead are provided to reveal to us our own intrinsic desire for violence, and especially how we place the blame for this violence upon God by making it "divinely-sanctioned" violence.

One place this is seen most clearly is in the sacrificial violence of the Bible.

CHAPTER 6

REVEALS THE TRUTH ABOUT SACRIFICE

The sacrificial system in Scripture is a perfect example of how we humans follow the violence that is in our hearts but blame it upon God. Since the sacrificial system is violence against animals (and sometimes humans) in order to earn God's favor and forgiveness, and since we never see Jesus Himself in the Gospel engage in such sacrificial violence, this is one area of Scripture which does more to reveal the heart of humanity to us than the heart of God.

We can begin to see this by comparing the commands in the Pentateuch for people to give blood sacrifices and burnt offerings to God with the numerous statements in the prophetical books which blatantly claim that God does not want blood sacrifices. For example, Jeremiah says that God never commanded His people to offer sacrifices and burnt offerings (Jer 7:22-23). Amos writes that God hated their religious festivals and burnt offerings (Amos 5:21-24). Micah points out that God doesn't need thousands of rams and rivers of oil, and definitely not a family's firstborn son. Instead, God wants justice, kindness, and humility (Mic 6:6-8). Even the Psalmist weighs in, saying that God is not delighted with sacrifices and offerings, but with a broken and contrite spirit (Ps 51:16-17).

Typically, pastors, professors, and Bible scholars fall into one of two camps on this issue. The first group sees all these statements as contradictions and so concludes that the Bible is not inerrant. Sometimes, rather than talking about contradictions in Scripture, they say instead that the Bible should be viewed more like a symphony, where each biblical author provides a unique perspective on the issues of their day, which may disagree with other voices, but when all are taken together, create a beautiful masterpiece. In this perspective, the Bible is a unified book only in that it is a conversation between diverse and disagreeing voices.

A second group of Bible teachers, however, holds firmly to the inerrancy of Scripture and filters all biblical interpretations through this grid. Since they are not willing or able to admit any sort of error or contradiction in the Bible, they say that God really did want the sacrifices and offerings that are commanded in the Pentateuch, and that the Prophets were only critical of the *attitude* or *spirit* in which the sacrifices were performed. They argue that the problem with the sacrifices is not that they were performed, but that God wanted them to be accompanied with justice, kindness, and humility in order to be effective.

The truth about sacrifice, however, is not found in either explanation. The first explanation argues that God does not want sacrifice. While true, this does not mean that the passages in the Old Testament are in error. Though they do not reveal the heart of God to us, these passages do reveal the heart of humanity to us. Furthermore, while the second explanation is correct in that the Bible is inerrant, it is incorrect in thinking that the entire Bible clearly reveals the heart of God to us.

Many texts, such as the sacrificial texts, actually reveal the heart of man to us.

How do they do that and what is it they reveal? The sacrificial texts reveal what we all see in our lives. The sacrificial instinct is alive and well in all of us, and though this instinct comes from within us, we believe it comes from God. The steps we take, the emotions we feel, and the logic we use in a sacrificial ritual are something all of us have experienced and each of us knows intuitively. When we sin, we feel guilt and shame. Since we feel upset and angry about our sin, we assume that God also must be angry. To alleviate this guilt and shame and the anger we think God has toward us, we often make a "sacrifice" of some sort to make God love us once again.

The sacrifice might be something as simple as not eating meat for a month, or punishing ourselves with mental, emotional, or even physical self-flagellation. We instinctively believe that payment is required for sin, and so when we sin, we try to make a payment for whatever it is we did. More importantly, however, this payment, or "sacrifice," usually makes us "feel better." This sense of feeling better makes us think that God also must feel better about us now that we have done something "good" to cover over the "bad." We assume the feelings of guilt and shame came upon us because God was angry with us for our sin, and therefore, the feelings of forgiveness as a result of sacrifice must have also came from God because He accepted our sacrifice.

Later, when we sin again, we remember what happened previously and how we alleviated our guilt by balancing out our sin with some sort of good work or sacrifice. Since the sacrifice or offerings seemed to work before, we once again turn to sacrifice and offerings as means of alleviating guilt and shame. If, however, the sacrifice doesn't work and we feel no forgiveness, we believe that maybe God wants a greater sacrifice, one with more value. We believe that God is now angrier with us because we keep committing the same sin, and so the same old sacrifice just isn't going to "work" the way it did before. So we up the ante and make a greater sacrifice to get God's attention and earn His forgiveness once again. This is one reason why some people groups in ancient times sacrificed virgins or firstborn sons, and why some people today give up jobs, possessions, or even turn away from family members. They do these things for the sake of gaining God's forgiveness. We make sacrifices to earn God's mercy and grace.

But as we have seen in Jesus, God does not need sacrifices in order to offer forgiveness. God's grace and love are not conditional upon the sacrifices we make. As Jesus revealed through His entire life and on the cross, God has always been freely forgiving and freely loving.

So why does the Bible say that God commanded people to make sacrifices? The reason the Bible says that God wants sacrifices is the same reason the people in the Gospels said that God wanted them to kill Jesus: Not because God did, but because the people wanted such things to alleviate their own guilt, shame, and fear.

Note carefully that when we project the guilt, shame, and fear that comes from our own heart onto the nature and character of God, so that we imagine that the guilt and shame we feel actually comes from God's shame and displeasure toward us, what we have actually done is make God in our own image. This revelation provides great insight into the nature and character of humanity.

CHAPTER 7

REVEALS THE TRUTH ABOUT HUMANS

The Non-Violent view of the atonement also reveals something crucial about humanity which is not found in any other atonement theory. Understanding humanity begins with understanding that we eventually become like what we worship. If we worship a God who is made in the image of sinful man, we will become more sinful, not less. But if we recognize that many elements of the image of God in the Old Testament are based on what man is like instead of what God is like, it is then that we are freed to take an honest look at ourselves and at God. If Jesus reveals to us what God is like, then if we worship the God whom Jesus revealed, we will truly begin to become more like God. And in this way, we will begin to become more truly human as well. Just as Jesus is the lens through which we understand God and the Bible, Jesus is also the lens through which we begin to understand what God intends humanity to be like. In the same way that Jesus reveals to us what God is like and how to read the Old Testament to see what humanity is like, so also, Jesus on the cross reveals to us what mankind is *supposed* to be like. If the Old Testament reveals the truth about mankind's problem, Jesus reveals the truth about mankind's potential.

If Jesus were a human like any other human, or even if Jesus was a god like any other god, as He hung on the cross He would have cried out for vengeance and retaliation. But He did not. He cried out for forgiveness. In this way, we not only see that God has always been forgiving humanity for our sins against Him, but also that this is how God wants each of us as humans to behave toward those who sin against us. In Jesus, God did not behave like a human would, but rather showed us how a human could behave. He provided a brand new vision for a new humanity, a template for the type of people God knows we can be. On the cross, Jesus not only reveals God to us, but He also reveals mankind to us, both the mankind we *have* become (as sinners who blame God and others for our sin) and the mankind we *can* become (as people who forgive others for their sin in order to stop the cycle of violence).

Jesus' death on the cross "in the name of God" reveals the truth to us about the violence done in Scripture at the hands of men "in the name of God." The violence of God in the Bible is human violence projected onto God. Examples include the Canaanite genocide, the declarations of war against God's enemies, and all killing of others in God's name. We made God appear to be violent as a means to justify our own violence. Jesus came to reveal that the source of divine violence is the human heart and that all so-called "justified violence" is nothing more than violence that we justify by claiming that God is on our side against our enemies.

Note very carefully that if God truly engaged in violence against human sinners, He never would have let us kill His Son, or at least, He never would have let us get away with it. If God were as violent toward sinful humanity as many Old Testament texts portray Him to be, He would have lashed out in anger and retaliation against the greatest sin of all, the sin of God's created beings killing God's only begotten Son. But since God revealed Himself in Jesus to be someone who always loves and only forgives, then we are able to clearly see that the violence that put Jesus on the cross was not divine violence, but human violence projected upon God.

This is why violence is the most prominent theme in the Old Testament. No human activity is mentioned as frequently in the Old Testament as the activity of violence. Raymund Schwager states that the Old Testament books "contain over six hundred passages that explicitly talk about nations, kings, or individuals attacking, destroying, and killing others. ... No other human activity or experience is mentioned as often."[1] Yet for all the examples of human violence, references to divine violence appear almost twice as often. Again, Schwager provides the statistics:

> The theme of God's bloody vengeance occurs in the Old Testament even more frequently than the problem of human violence. Approximately one thousand passages speak of Yahweh's blazing anger. ... No other topic is as often mentioned as God's bloody works. A theology of the Old Testament revelation that does not specifically deal with this grave and somber fact misses from the very start one of the most central questions ..."[2]

A straightforward reading of the Old Testament text seems to indicate that as violent as humanity can be, God outdoes us all;

---

[1] Raymund Schwager, *Must There Be Scapegoats? Violence and Redemption in the Bible* (New York: Crossroad, 2000), 47.

[2] Ibid., 55.

God is more bloody and violent than all humanity combined. If this is the case, is it any wonder that humans are murderously violent—just like their God in whose image and likeness they are made? Between the violence of humanity and violence of God, it is obvious that "violence is the most central theme in the Old Testament."[3]

What we learn from Jesus' experience on the cross is that the reason God appears so violent in Scripture is because we humans are the violent ones, but we blame God for our violence. God is the divine scapegoat for human violence. The Old Testament is so violent because the Old Testament is God helping us see into our own hearts. The violence of Scripture is human violence (that we project upon God) staring us in the face. Despite all our scholarship, studies, and sermons, we have missed the main revelation of the Bible. Though we want the Bible to be "a morally reassuring manual of religious piety"[4] The Bible we want is not the Bible God gave us. We have completely ignored the main truth of Scripture, and especially the main truth of the Old Testament text when read through a crucivision lens.

And what truth is that? The truth that we are the violent ones, and there is no violence in God at all. The truth that God appears violent because we have made Him to be the scapegoat for our own violence. The truth is that God appears violent to us only because we do not want to admit our own violence and so we blame Him for it. "It is men, not God, who have produced racks, whips, prisons, slavery, guns, bayonets, and

---

[3] Ibid., 66.

[4] Gil Bailie, *Violence Unveiled: Humanity at the Crossroads* (New York: Crossroad, 2013), 135.

bombs,"[5] but we tend to blame God for these anyway, and especially for how we use these instruments of violence against others. In our scapegoating violence we have made God the universal scapegoat for all violence. The truth is that the reason the God of the Bible engages in so much violence is not because He is violent, but because we are violent and we justify this violence by blaming God it. This is both why violence is the most prominent theme in all of Scripture and why most of this violence is attributed to God.

We have, each one of us, like Cain, killed our brothers. And the blood of every victim in Scripture and in history cries out from the ground. And when God appears and says, "What have you done?" we reply, along with Cain, that we are the victims, that we are the ones God has wronged, that if He would treat us more fairly, life would turn out better.

In our hearts, we secretly desire to become God. We secretly believe that if we were running the world, we could do a better job than God. In our hearts, we secretly imagine that God has wronged us, not treated us fairly, and has shown favoritism to others. And so we grow in our resentment towards God. We secretly wish that we could replace God. With this secret desire in our hearts, we set out to "be God" to the world by doing the things He doesn't seem to be doing. We try to make things right. We try to enact justice. We try to retaliate against wrongdoers when God doesn't.

So while our rivalry is outwardly against our brother, it is inwardly against God. Our ultimate rival is God Himself. If we were God, we would accept the human offerings of fruit so that

---

[5] C. S. Lewis, *The Problem of Pain* (New York: Collier, 1962), Chapter 4, Human Pain.

humanity could return to the garden. But since He does not accept our offerings, the problem must lie with someone else, or even with God Himself. The original lie in the Garden of Eden was that God withheld good things from us. This is the same lie that caused Cain to kill his brother and the lie we believe today when we murder others in the name of God. We feel we must do God's job for Him because He is not doing the good in this world as He should. Like Cain, we feel that we must be the saviors of the world, and this requires that we stop anyone who gets in our way. After all, we are only doing God's will as we attempt to save the human family from sin and separation from God. In our desire to save humanity, we usurp the place of God.

When God sees the desire to be God well up in our hearts, He warns us. "Be careful! Sin is crouching at your door!" But we see the sin only in our brother, and we try to protect ourselves from this sin by "righteously" killing "God's rivals," who are really only our rivals. It is "they," not "us," who are withholding our family from returning to the Garden. It is "they," not "us," who keep us from experiencing peace and prosperity from God. And ultimately, it is God Himself who is not behaving rightly as He should (or as we would in His position), and so we must take God's responsibilities upon ourselves because He seems to have abandoned His post.

When we place ourselves as the bringers of peace, as God's spokesman in the world, as the ones who will restore humanity to the garden, and then God seems to favor someone else who is "doing it all wrong," we get jealous and envious. We set out to kill and destroy them so that we ourselves do not lose our privileged position. This desire to be God leads to a rivalry against others, which leads to murdering our rivals, as we think God should do.

Thus goes Scripture and history. We behave violently toward others and then blame God for it. When we see violence in this world, we look at God and say, "God, what have you done?" But in Scripture, when we ask God why He allows such violence, God look at us and says, "What have you done?" God is not seeking to blame us as we blame Him. No, God wants us to see our collusion with violence and especially how we have engaged in violence in His name. Once we have seen this, He wants us to turn from victimizing violence and become catalysts for grace in a violent world. Along with sending Jesus into this world to deal with sin and violence, God's response and solution to sin and violence is to send *us* as agents of healing, grace, mercy, forgiveness, and reconciliation. When we fail or refuse to act as God's agents of healing, we tend to blame God for our failures. When we say, "God, where were you?" His answer is always, "Where were *you?*"

Our response, however, is that of Cain's. We try to turn the blame back on God. We say, "Don't punish me. It was you. You drove me away. If you would only treat me fairly, I would not have had to do what I did. I got a bad hand in life. I was not treated rightly. If I had not done what was necessary, I would not have received what was rightfully mine." Like Cain (and Adam before him), we have always blamed God. We blame Him for not running the world correctly. We blame Him for not killing our rivals. We blame Him for not setting things straight in the world.

Note again that if God behaved like a human, He would set out to prove His innocence. He would set out to kill us in retaliation for trying to take His place, for trying to be a rival to God, for questioning how He runs the world, and for killing others in His name when He had nothing to do with such evil. But in Jesus, we see that God is not like a human, nor is God like the god we imagined Him to be. On the cross, when faced with all the blame for our sin and shame, God did not defend Himself or retaliate for the wrong done to Him or in His name. Instead, God bore the blame and took the shame. Though innocent of any wrongdoing, God, in Jesus, let us blame Him for every wrongdoing.

And then He let us kill Him in God's name.

Again, this goes back to Cain. Why did we kill Jesus? For the same reason Cain killed Abel. To set things right. To restore order. To defend God's righteousness. To bring justice. We were the ones who had the plan to set things right and bring humanity back into Paradise. We religious people knew what God wanted and how He wanted it. We believed we knew how we had offended God, and what was necessary to appease Him. But the teachings and example of Jesus messed everything up, and when it appeared that God favored Jesus more than all our religious rules, regulations, and restrictions, we knew that He had to be stopped. We brought our unwanted, unneeded, and unasked-for offerings of fruit in order to please and appease a God who was not angry at us in the first place. And when we saw that our brother, Jesus, was accepted by God, we became jealous, and so we killed Him.

Yet though the blood of Abel cried out from the ground for vengeance, the blood of Jesus cries out from the cross for forgiveness. The sin of the first man, Adam, brought about the murder of brother against brother and a never-ending cycle of retaliatory vengeance. The offering of the second Man, Jesus, also brought about the murder of brother against brother (and of man against God), but instead of vengeance, Jesus offered a word of forgiveness which showed the alternative to retaliation. Of all the murders in the world, God alone could have righteously retaliated for the unjust murder of His innocent Son, but instead, He forgave, showing that the only way to peace, love, and unity is through forgiveness.

The truth Jesus reveals on the cross about mankind is multi-faceted in both its grotesqueness and its beauty. It reveals first the depths of the depravity of mankind, that we are so murderously evil that we made God in our murderous image. Second, it reveals that just as God has always been forgiving us, the way to break out of our murderous evil and become truly human is not to respond to evil with evil but to respond with forgiveness and grace.

Yet even this is not all the cross reveals about mankind. If it is true, as we have seen again and again above, that God has always been loving us, forgiving us, and accepting us, then how can we explain the experience of human separation from God? To answer this, we must learn to see what the Non-Violent atonement reveals about sin.

CHAPTER 8

REVEALS THE TRUTH ABOUT SIN

Since Jesus defeated sin, death, and the devil through His crucifixion, it is no real surprise to learn that the Non-Violent view of the atonement reveals something critically important about sin. While all atonement theories have at their foundation the belief that mankind is sinful and therefore in need of atonement, the Non-Violent view of the atonement leads us to see something unique about the nature of this sin. The Non-Violent view of the atonement reveals where sin came from, what it does, and why it is so important for God to do something about it.

To see this, let us begin with how sin is traditionally presented in other views. Most views of the atonement give sin way too much power. Many people view sin almost as an all-consuming power which threatens the holiness of God if left unchecked. Some forms of popular theology almost view sin as a threat to God's rule over the universe. Though few, if any, would state this idea of sin as starkly or bluntly as I have here, such a view of sin is nevertheless at the foundation of much of today's theology. This is what lies behind the ominous warnings about keeping ourselves from sin because "God cannot look upon sin" or "sin cannot be in God's presence."

In the minds of some, this threat to God's righteous rule is so grave, God has no choice but to fight back against sin. But more than this, sin is so powerful, God has to make sure that in His battle against sin, He never draws too near to sin, or lets sin into His presence, or even looks upon sin, lest sin somehow taints God's perfect holiness. To hear some talk about sin, if only one sinner came into close proximity to God, sin would mar God's nature for all eternity and the universe would fall into the blackness of death forever.

Such a view of sin is complete rubbish, especially when viewed in light of the incarnation, crucifixion, and resurrection of Jesus.

If the incarnation, crucifixion, and resurrection of Jesus reveal anything at all about sin, it is that sin has absolutely no power over God whatsoever. Sin cannot taint God in any way, shape, or form. Sin cannot defeat God, or even put a scratch on His character. If it were true that sin cannot be in God's presence and that God cannot look upon sin, Jesus could not have been fully God yet still come to earth to live and eat with sinful human beings. But Jesus is fully God and He did come to this earth to live and eat with sinful human beings. More than that, on the cross, Jesus took all the sins of all people in all the world throughout all of history upon Himself, and in so doing, was not defeated by sin, but quite to the contrary, defeated sin instead!

To say that God cannot look upon sin or be in the presence of evil is to deny that Jesus was fully God. Did Jesus come to this earth? Of course! Did He ignore sin and keep Himself away from all who were sinners! Far from it! Rather, He sought out the sinners. He hung around the prostitutes and tax collectors. He laid hands on the lepers and showed love to adulterers. On the cross, Jesus took our sin upon Himself. Second Corinthians 5:21 even says that He became sin for us and Galatians 3:13 says He took the curse of sin upon Himself. He could have done none of this if sin had any chance of defeating God.

The Non-Violent view of the atonement shows how powerless sin truly is. While it is true that "God cannot look on sin" this is only because sin wilts and withers away at His gaze. While it is true that sin cannot be in the presence of a Holy God, this is only because the purifying fire of His infinite holiness washes away all sin in a torrent of love and grace. To say that sin could taint God is like saying that a drop of water could quench the sun. Sin cannot touch God because, just like a drop of water evaporates into nothingness before it gets within a million miles of the sun, so also, sin is burnt away into nothingness when God draws near.

The reason some say that God cannot look upon sin is because of what we read in Habakkuk 1:13: "Your eyes are too pure to look on evil; you cannot tolerate wrong" (NIV). But this is a text where the context is critically important (is there any other kind of text?). Following the statement, Habakkuk complains that God is looking upon sin and evil (Hab 1:14), and seems to be tolerating wickedness and evil because He is doing nothing about it. In this book, the prophet asks numerous questions to God about how God is running the world and handling Israel. The prophet Habakkuk looks around him at what is going on in the world and has trouble reconciling it with what He knows about God and so He asks a couple challenging questions about God's behavior and actions. Habakkuk 1:13 is the second of those questions, but it is related to the first question (Hab 1:2-4). Both questions deal with how God can allow sin to continue on in His world. Such questions of how there can be evil in God's world is one of the most frequently asked questions in history.

The context makes it clear that Habakkuk does not believe that God cannot see evil. To the contrary, Habakkuk knows that God sees everything that goes on in the world, including all evil. The rest of Scripture reveals this very thing. From the very beginning, God saw that Adam and Eve had sinned, and He saw when Cain killed His brother Abel, and He saw when the people on the earth became so wicked that a flood was going to destroy them all. We could go on and on throughout the Bible to see that God both knows the evil that is going on in the world and He sees it. God sees every bit of sin and evil in this world.

So to say that God cannot look upon sin is not accurate biblically and is not what Habakkuk 1:13 teaches. Instead, Habakkuk is saying that God, by not seeming to do anything about evil, appears to be looking upon evil *with approval*. But if we know that God does not look upon evil in approval but disapproves of it, how is it that the treacherous seem to live in God's favor and the wicked win at everything while the godly and the righteous suffer and die? This is the question that Habakkuk asks. If we look around in the world, we often have the same question. Why do the wicked prosper? Why do the treacherous thrive? (Jer 12:1). Job asked a similar question as well in Job 21:7.

God's answer to Habakkuk is the same answer we see in the person and work of Jesus Christ. He tells Habakkuk that sin is its own punishment (Hab 2:5-20). God tells Habakkuk that He doesn't have to do anything about sin, because sin eats and destroys those who continue to live in sin. God's job is to warn people of the devastating and disastrous consequences of sin

and to do what He can to protect people from these consequences, but if people persist in sin, the results of their sin will
eventually fall upon their own heads. Sin is punished, God
says, but God is not the one who does the punishing.

God's answer to evil is not what we think it should be. If we
were God, we would crush all evil and destroy all evildoers.
We only think this, however, because we do not see the condition of our own hearts, nor do we see the myriad ways we con-
tribute to the great evils in this world. God cannot crush and
destroy evil without crushing and destroying everybody in this
world. But neither does God stick His head in the sand and act
as if evil does not exist. God is doing something about evil. But
what God does about evil is so scandalous and shocking, we
often fail to recognize it. Far from averting His gaze, or keeping Himself separate from all the sin and evil in the world, God
dives right into the thick of it. He finds the vilest places, the
most terrible crimes, and the evilest situations, and jumps in.
This is what we see Him do in Jesus Christ.

This is hardly a God who appears scared about sin. This is
hardly a God who is so holy, He cannot touch evil. This is a
God for whom sin is so insignificant to Him and is such a mi-
nor concern, He doesn't think twice about entering the darkest
of places or the most sinful of people and taking up inhabitance
there.

Why?

Because He loves us too much to leave us in the darkness of
sin. Because the light shines brightest in the darkest of areas.

If Jesus reveals God to us, then we can assume that God also likes to hang out with sinners and show love to the wicked.
To say that God cannot look upon sin is to say that sin can defeat and defile God; that sin is more powerful than the righteous holiness of God. God is not so weak and powerless. It is

precisely because God *can* look upon sin that He sent His son Jesus Christ to do something about sin, and it is only because God *can* be in the presence of sin that He is able to be with each one of us in the midst of our sin and filth. God loves us so much, He is willing to walk with us and be near us through the worst of our sins.

This is clearly revealed once again in what God did through Jesus on the cross. On the cross, Jesus became sin for us (2 Cor 5:20-21). Why? Not so that sin could consume Him, but so that He could consume sin. And why did He do this? Because sin was consuming us, and He loved us so much. Jesus took consuming sin upon Himself so that He might deliver us from its deathly power. Jesus took the sin of the world upon Himself, so that the tidal waves of its power might fall upon Him and evaporate away into nothingness before His holiness. In taking sin upon Himself, Jesus defeated sin by washing it away and releasing those who were held captive to it.

> The [Non-Violent] or social theory of the atonement ... proclaimed release of the captives to those who had formerly been deluded and enslaved by the Domination System, and it set itself against that system with all its might.[1]

God fights against sin, not because it is a threat to Him, but because it is a threat to us. God is not on His throne, getting angry at us every time we sin. God is not shaking His head, saying, "I can't believe he did that again! One more time and I will squash him like a bug!" No, that is not the God that Jesus revealed. When we sin, God is not surprised. He is not

---

[1] Walter Wink, *Engaging the Powers: Discernment and Resistance in a World of Domination* (Minneapolis: Fortress, 1992), 150.

shocked. Nor is He embarrassed by what we have done. Our sin does not cause God to turn away from us in shame. God saw our sin coming from billions of years away and He still sent Jesus to this earth because He loves us. God does not hate us because we sin. He loves us in our sin. His love for us will not change and is always enough to cover all our sin.

Therefore, sin simply isn't an issue with God. The sin of humanity, as great as it is, is less than a tiny speck of sand in the vast ocean of God's loving-kindness and grace. Yes, sin is a problem, but it is not a problem for God; sin is a problem for us. While sin saddens and grieves God, this is only because He sees how much sin hurts us. Sin hurts people. It enslaves families. It destroys lives. It ruins relationships. When these things happen as a result of sin, God is grieved. As a loving parent, God does not want His children to experience pain and suffering caused by sin. This is why He warns us in Scripture against sin. Sin damages us, and God does not want to see us damaged. The pain and suffering we experience from sin is not because God is inflicting us with punishment for sin, but because pain and suffering are the natural consequence of sin.

This ultimately is the truth about sin that Jesus revealed on the cross. God is not angry about our sin, but He is angry at the damage that sin does to us. Sin is a problem, not because it is a problem for God, but because it is a problem for us. Sin hurts us, and since God loves us, He seeks to do something about sin for us. He has taken our sin and shame upon Himself. He has died for our sin. He has let us blame Him for our sin. And ultimately, finally, through a gruesome death on the cross, He has shown us where sin leads. Sin always and only leads to death. And while God begs with us and pleads with us to keep from sinning, and does everything He can to protect us from the devastating consequences of sin, the natural consequences of sin leads to death and destruction in the same way that jumping off a cliff leads to nothing but blood and broken bones at the bottom. God always forgives and always extends grace, but even forgiveness and grace cannot always keep us from experiencing the consequences of sin.

When Christians hear that God forgives unconditionally and extends grace without limit, they often object to such an idea by saying, "So people can just go sin all they want?" Asking this question is like asking, "So people can just go jump off cliffs?" The answer of course, is "Yes ... if that is really what they want to do." If you really want to stab yourself in the leg, you can, but it will *really* hurt. Similarly, if you want to commit adultery, you can, but it will likely destroy your marriage, your finances, your life, your children, and maybe even your health and your job. God will forgive you for adultery and extend His grace to those who live this way, but the consequences that follow adultery are well-known and unavoidable. This is why God warns against adultery.

This is very similar to what Paul is saying in Romans 6. When someone objects to Paul's teaching about grace by asking if they can sin all they want so that grace may abound (Rom 6:1; 15), Paul's answer does not mean, as many claim, that "true Christians cannot continue in sin." What Paul means is that people who understand what sin does simply do not want to continue in it. When Paul says, "God Forbid!" he is not saying, "No, you cannot!" but rather, "Why would you want to?"

If the death of Jesus for the sins of the whole world reveals anything at all, it proves to us that no amount of sin can ever separate us from the love of God. Furthermore, the death of Jesus on the cross reveals that God will do everything He can to rescue us from the devastating and destructive consequences of sin. The death of Jesus on the cross reveals that sin hurts. It ruins lives, destroys relationships, bankrupts finances, separates marriages, loses jobs, shortens longevity, twists emotions, and damages the psyche.

But even if we choose to abuse grace in this way, and test the forgiveness and longsuffering of God, will He still forgive us? Yes, of course He will. God freely and forever forgives all people of all sin. This shocking truth about forgiveness is another truth that was revealed by Jesus on the cross.

CHAPTER 9

REVEALS THE TRUTH ABOUT FORGIVENESS

On the cross, as humans were in the very act of committing the greatest crime in human history, Jesus revealed to us the heart of God for humanity regarding our sin. He cried out, "Father, forgive them, for they know not what they do" (Luke 23:34). If this is the cry of Jesus regarding the ultimate crime of the murder of God, does this not mean that God has a heart filled with forgiveness for all other sins as well? If God forgave us while we killed His Son, will He not also forgive us for all our other sins as well, no matter how grievous (cf. Rom 5:8; 8:31-39)?

We often get confused about what the Bible teaches about forgiveness because some texts seem to teach that forgiveness is conditional upon confession, repentance, or forgiving others for their sin against us (cf. Matt 6:15; Matt 18:35; Luke 3:4; 24:47; Acts 2:38; 1 John 1:9). But then there are texts which teach that God extends unconditional and free forgiveness to all people without restriction (cf. 2 Cor 2:7, 10; Col 2:13). When we read these apparently contradictory texts, we are left wondering whether God really forgives us or not.

The solution to this problem is to recognize that there are two kinds of forgiveness in the Bible. The first kind of forgiveness comes from the Greek word *charizomai*. The word means "to give" in the sense of giving something freely to someone that they do not deserve and did not earn. This makes sense, because this type of forgiveness is based on the word *charis*, which means "grace." When used in the context of how God deals with sin, it refers to "God's unconditional forgiveness." *Charizomai* refers to the removal of guilt, but not necessarily the removal of consequences. *Charizomai* is God's free pardon (cf. 2 Cor 2:7, 10; Col 2:13). As such, *charizomai* is offered freely, to all, with absolutely no conditions. This kind of forgiveness is a free gift of God to every single person on earth, emanating purely from God's love and grace. Because of *charizomai*, all people have been forgiven for every sin, without exception.

The second kind of forgiveness comes from the Greek word *aphesis* (Another word used for this kind of forgiveness is *apoluō*). While the word forgiveness is often used to translate the word *aphesis*, it is best to think of *aphesis* as "release." It is used to refer to the release of a financial debt or burden, but is often used in the sense of gaining liberty or freedom from captivity, slavery, or bondage. Unlike *charizomai*, however, *aphesis* usually has conditions. While *charizomai* forgiveness is unconditional, *aphesis* forgiveness is not. *Aphesis* forgiveness usually comes as a result of confession, repentance, or forgiving others (cf. Matt 6:15; Matt 18:35; Luke 3:4; 24:47; Acts 2:38; 1 John 1:9).

This makes sense when we understand that sin enslaves us and puts us in bondage. If we do not repent of our sin, if we do not turn away from it and turn back toward God, how can we gain freedom, liberty, or release from it? We cannot. While

God freely forgives us for all our sins (*charizomai*), if we want to experience freedom and release from the captivating power of sin (*aphesis*) we must agree that we have sinned (confess) and turn from such behavior to start following God (repentance). Even if we do not gain *aphesis*, we still have *charizomai* from God. He freely forgives us out of His grace, and calls us to repent so that we might also gain *aphesis*. If we do not, He still loves us and forgives us (*charizomai*), but we will continue to experience bondage and enslavement to sin.

Armed with this understanding of the two types of forgiveness, we can begin to understand why the Bible seems to have two messages about forgiveness. When forgiveness seems to be conditional upon confession, repentance, or forgiving others, it usually has *aphesis* forgiveness in mind. When, however, the forgiveness seems to be freely offered with no strings attached, it usually has *charizomai* forgiveness in view.

Some people object that when Jesus cried out for God to forgive those who were crucifying Him, He asked for *aphesis* (Luke 23:34). Wouldn't this be the perfect example of where *charizomai* should be offered? Yes, it would, except for three reasons. The first reason that Jesus asked God for *aphesis* forgiveness instead of *charizomai* is because God has always extended *charizomai*. The death of Jesus was not where *charizomai* began, and the death of Jesus is not what bought or enabled the *charizomai* of God. To ask for *charizomai* would have given us the wrong impression about what Jesus was doing on the cross. If Jesus had asked for *charizomai*, Jesus would have asked for something that God has already extended. There has never been a time when God's free and gracious forgiveness has not been extended. Due to a warped understanding of sin and forgiveness, some people have the idea that God only started to truly forgive people after Jesus died on the cross. But this is not true. On the cross, Jesus revealed to the world what God has always been like. Jesus did not ask God for *charizomai* on the cross because God was already extending *charizomai* to all people for all sins. Asking God to extend *charizomai* would have been like asking God to make the sky blue or to let people breathe oxygen. This is why Jesus asked for the conditional forgiveness of *aphesis* instead.

The second reason Jesus asked God for *aphesis* is indicated by the implied condition in Jesus' request for forgiveness. What condition? Those who crucified Him did not know what they were doing. They were sinning in ignorance. The specific sin they were committing was the sin of scapegoating, the sin which has been hidden since the foundation of the world (Matt 13:35), but which Jesus was now unveiling to all. This does not mean that Jesus would not have asked for forgiveness if the people had actually known what they were doing. No, it simply means that in this instance, they sinned out of ignorance, which led to Jesus asking God to extend *aphesis* forgiveness to them. Jesus knew there could be disastrous consequences for murdering the Son of God, and Jesus asked God to release the people from these consequences because they did not know what they were doing.

The third reason that Jesus asked for *aphesis* is related to this. Because they sinned in ignorance, Jesus wanted to do everything possible to protect the people from the disastrous and devastating consequences of their sin. This is what *aphesis* does. Sin always has consequences, but God, in His mercy and grace, does everything He can to protect us from the consequences of our sin. As a good Father, He seeks to spare us pain. This is especially true when we sin in ignorance, as was the case with the crucifixion of Jesus. But when we sin knowingly, and we continue to sin knowingly, despite all warnings of what will happen, there comes a time when God must allow the consequences of our sin to catch up with us so that we can learn through the pain of experience what happens when we act contrary to His will. In such cases, it is not God punishing us, but our sin. Sin promises pleasure, which it often provides, but this pleasure often comes with a hefty price of pain. If we continue in sin after being warned repeatedly to turn from our ways, God, as our loving Father, lets sin have its way with us so that we can learn from our mistakes before some greater pain falls upon us.

So even *aphesis* forgiveness is often freely and graciously extended from God. God does not send pain, suffering, and punishment upon us because of our sin, but tries to protect us, not only from sin, but primarily from the destructive consequences of sin in our lives. This nearly limitless *aphesis* forgiveness is what Jesus told His disciples to extend to others in Matthew 18. Certain religious teachers in the days of Jesus taught that forgiveness should be extended three times to those who repeatedly sin against you, but after that you had no obligation to forgive. After Jesus taught about forgiveness, Peter asked Jesus how many times they must forgive (He uses the word *aphesis*). Peter suggested that seven times was enough (Matt 18:21-22). Apparently, Peter doubled the amount of forgiveness that was recommended by the religious leaders of his day, and then added one more for good measure.

In response, Jesus said that seven times was not enough, but seventy times seven. Does this mean that after we forgive someone 490 times, forgiveness no longer needs to be extended? No. It means that we must not keep count when forgiving others. We must, as Paul says in 1 Corinthians 13, keep no record of wrongs, but must always love and always forgive. Jesus' instruction about forgiveness, even *aphesis* forgiveness, shows us what kind of *aphesis* God extends toward us. If God is the example we are to follow, and if Jesus is the exact representation of God, and if Jesus says that we must forgive others without limit, then it follows that God forgives without limit as well, even when it comes to *aphesis* forgiveness.

Following this teaching about *aphesis* forgiveness in Matthew 18, Jesus tells a parable about an unforgiving servant who receives great forgiveness from his master but refuses to show forgiveness to someone ese. This parable shows that there are conditions to *aphesis*, and one of them is that we learn to show *aphesis* forgiveness to others as we have been freely given *aphesis* by God. If we are forgiven, yet refuse to forgive, then God will teach us the value of our forgiveness by allowing some of the consequences of our own failures to fall upon our heads. Just as God is ready, willing, and able to forgive us our sins, so also, we must be ready, willing, and able to forgive others (cf. Matt 6:12).

This truth about forgiveness is further amplified when we see what the Non-Violent view of the atonement reveals about justice.

CHAPTER 10

REVEALS THE TRUTH ABOUT JUSTICE

Despite all the teaching about forgiveness from Jesus and the cry of forgiveness that Jesus uttered from the cross, we often get the impression that God did not want to forgive people for their numerous sins against Him, but was persuaded or convinced to do so by Jesus. This is especially true when the cross of Jesus is viewed through the lens of retributive justice and the Penal Substitution view of the atonement. Deep in the heart of humanity is the feeling that God is angry with us about our sin and that God demands sacrifice to satisfy His anger. We interpret the cross of Jesus as the event where God demanded the blood of a perfect sacrifice to satisfy or placate His wrath toward sin. The way it is sometimes presented at a popular level, God was so angry about sin, He demanded death as a means to satisfy His wrath. But He also loved us, and so while justice demanded that He kill us all for our sin, He sought other methods of appeasement. Initially He required the blood of bulls and goats, though He knew that this was not a permanent solution. Instead, these sacrifices only looked forward to the death of His Son, Jesus, upon whom He poured His wrath so that it would not fall upon us. As a result of this narrative, some people have an impression of God as being so angry about sin, that He just had to kill somebody, and rather than take out His anger on all of us, He killed Jesus instead. God required payment for forgiveness, and took temporary payments from the blood of bulls and goats until He was able to receive full payment through the blood of Jesus, at which point He was able to finally extend forgiveness of sins.

We have already seen in previous sections of this book that God was not angry at humanity for our sin and did not demand sacrifice as a way of getting payment for our sin, and so the truth about forgiveness is now easier to see: God did not need or want to kill anyone or anything in order to extend forgiveness. Both types of forgiveness are freely extended by God without payment of any kind. Though *aphesis* does often have conditions, the achievement of these conditions do nothing to please or appease God, but simply help us avoid the dire consequences of our own sin.

This truth about the freedom of forgiveness is seen more clearly when we think about the price of forgiveness. Forgiveness, by definition, does not require payment. If your neighbor has wronged you and you eventually decide to forgive him, do you first need to make him pay for what he has done? Of course not! You can just forgive him. If you ask for restitution and receive it, then you are not forgiving him, but are getting paid to not retaliate in kind, which is not forgiveness at all. You cannot demand payment when someone wrongs you as a condition for forgiveness because then it is not forgiveness. You can either get paid off or you can forgive, but you cannot do both.

Worse yet would be making someone else pay for the wrong your neighbor has done to you. If you are angry at your neighbor for something he did, and your son comes to you and says, "Don't hurt the neighbor; hurt me instead," would following your son's suggestion do anything to help relieve your anger toward the neighbor at all? No. Abusing your own son would do nothing to alleviate your anger toward your neighbor. If you want to forgive your neighbor for a wrong done to you, the only way to forgive is to simply forgive. No payment by him, or an innocent third party, is required.

Therefore, if it is insisted that divine forgiveness requires payment of some sort, then we must conclude that God never really forgives anyone. Instead, He gets paid off. While payment for sin might *satisfy* God, such satisfaction is the opposite of forgiveness. If a debt is cancelled by being paid off, then there is no need for forgiveness. You cannot call something "forgiveness" if the debt was paid off. Let us say you have a loan from the bank and you cannot make your payments, so you call the bank to see if they will forgive your debt. How would you respond if they say, "Sure! We'll forgive your debt as soon as you pay off your loan." Is that forgiveness? Of course not.

Yet how often we hear it preached that "God is a God of forgiveness; but He is also a God of justice. So before God can forgive, the debt of sin must be paid!" These Bible teachers then go on to say that since God is just, someone had to pay the penalty for our sin and so the wrath of God toward sin was poured out upon Jesus. The idea is that God was just toward Jesus (who bore our sin) so that He might be merciful and forgiving toward us.

Again, this sounds right and logical until we realize that forgiveness is incompatible with justice. Forgiveness is not the other side of the coin of justice; but the exact opposite. One cannot forgive and demand justice at the same time. If you forgive someone, you cannot then turn around and demand that they (or someone else) receive the punishment they deserve. Nor can you punish someone for what they did and then turn around and say you extended "forgiveness." When someone does something bad, and you are in a position to make them suffer consequences for their behavior, you can either give them justice or forgiveness, but you cannot do both. Once justice is served, forgiveness is no longer needed, and vice versa.

Take an example from life. Imagine someone robs a bank. They get arrested and go to court. However sorry the thief is, it is unlikely that the judge will forgive him and let him go. This is not what judges do. Judges do not forgive people; they judge people. So in this instance, the judge gives the bank robber 20 years in prison. This is justice. Twenty years later, when the robber is released from prison, can the judge meet this man at the prison gates and say, "I forgive you for what you did, and so you can now get out of jail?" Of course not! After the prison sentence was served, justice has been done and the opportunity for forgiveness is long gone. The criminal served his time and is now getting out of jail as a result of justice, not as a result of forgiveness.

This is also how it works when we sin against God. When our sins are brought before Him, He can either serve justice or forgiveness, but not both. This is even true if God's justice was put upon Jesus. If Jesus paid the demands of justice, then God does not extend forgiveness. If the death of Jesus on the cross was for the purpose of meeting the demands of justice, then justice has been served and forgiveness does not enter the picture. If, however, God decided to forgive mankind, then He eliminates the need for justice. God can either forgive or demand justice, but He cannot do both.

In light of this, it can be argued that sometimes forgiveness is *true* justice. While justice is often blind to the specific circumstances of a crime and to the loving application of the law, forgiveness is often extended in light of extenuating circumstances or an understanding of the intent of the law. But justice never takes such things into consideration and often follows the letter of the law, even if such an application of the law is inherently unjust. It is true that "every pursuit of justice not only rests on partial justice but also creates new injustices."[1] This is because justice never allows for things like love, relationship, or friendship to enter into the equation of how justice is served. A just judge is supposed to be impartial and fair, treating everyone equally whether they are the world's worst criminal or his very own child. A just judge is supposed to hand down the same sentence for a particular crime no matter what reasons the person had for committing that crime. A just judge only cares about what the law says; he does not (indeed, *cannot*) care about the person who broke the law. The judgments of a judge who cares about the person on the bench cannot usually be trusted.

But God does care. He cares deeply. He wants to have a deep personal relationship with each and every person on the bench. He sees each man and woman as His very own child and He loves them more than His own life. Because of His great love for each guilty person, He does not want to see pure justice served; He wants mercy and forgiveness to be extended. As such, God is not a just judge. Instead, He is a merciful, forgiving, and loving Father. He knows the extenuating circum-

---

[1] Friedrich Nietzsche, summarized by Miroslav Volf in Brad Jersak and Michael Hardin, eds., *Stricken by God? Nonviolent Identification and the Victory of Christ* (Grand Rapids: Eerdmans, 2007), 269.

stances. He knows all the small mistakes that led up to the co-
lossal crime. He knows that there was a tempter whispering lies
in our ears. He knows about the absent parents, the financial
crisis, the health concern, the need for acceptance, the threat of
starvation, the depression, the anger, the strife, the poverty, the
abusive relationship, or whatever else might have led up to the
accused person making the decision they did. He sees. He
knows. He understands. And He looks at us and says, "I will
have mercy on whomever I will have mercy, and I will have
compassion on whomever I will have compassion (Rom 9:15).
I pronounce you 'Not Guilty.' You are forgiven. You are set
free." This reveals the truth once again of what we saw earlier,
that "To know all is to forgive all."

> God's judgment is never simply justice. In terms of straightfor-
> ward legal thinking, God is much too lenient or merciful. God is
> patient and "slow to anger" and open to changing the divine
> mind (see Jonah 3:8-10; 4:2). Judgment is understood in relation-
> al terms; a relationship is at stake, not an agreement or a contract
> or a set of rules. The personal/relational dimension of judgment,
> not unlike the relationship between a parent and child, sharply
> qualifies any strictly legal or juridical understandings.
>
> God is not at all a neutral party in these matters or an objective
> representative of an independent court of justice (such as a typi-
> cal judge would be). Again, God is more like a parent, openly
> anguished over what to do about a wayward child (e.g., Hosea
> 6:4, "What shall I do with you?" and 11:1-9). What would court-
> rooms be like if judges were to display such personal anguish
> and anger? To mix metaphors, if God is viewed as the divine
> judge behind the bench, remember that God is also the spouse of

the accused one in the dock! Objectivity or neutrality goes out the door![2]

No prosecuting attorney in the world would allow this, of course. A judge cannot just ignore the law, no matter how loving and compassionate he wants to be toward the guilty party. The law is the law and it must be upheld, no matter what extenuating circumstances there might be. This same objection holds true in God's courtroom. But who is he that condemns? It is not Jesus Christ, for although He could condemn us, He is instead interceding for us before the throne of God (Rom 8:34). No, the only one who condemns is the devil. Satan is the accuser of the brethren (Rev 12:10). In the divine courtroom, Satan is the prosecuting attorney demanding that justice be served instead of mercy. It is Satan reminding God of the "righteous requirements of the law" that must be upheld lest all creation fall into anarchy and chaos.

All this is to say that any religious teaching which portrays God as an angry, vengeful deity whose primary concern is that people obey His law and those who do not must be severely punished, are not presenting the God revealed in Jesus Christ, but are instead representing a false deity which more closely resembles Satan. The god of retributive justice, who is morally obligated to punish those who transgress his rules and laws, is not the God revealed in Jesus Christ, but is a god who has its origin in satanic lies.

To put it more bluntly, although Jesus said that He has revealed to us what God is like, many religious people seem to think that God is more like Satan than Jesus. We often get our

---

[2] Terence E. Fretheim, *Creation Untamed: The Bible, God, and Natural Disasters* (Grand Rapids: Baker, 2010), 48-49.

ideas about Satan from fantasy literature, Hollywood movies, a few misunderstood biblical texts, and probably from Satan himself. He wants us to believe wrong things about who he is and what he does. Scripture doesn't say a whole lot about the devil, but what it does say is not accurately presented in most churches or popular-level Christian books. It is best to think of Satan not primarily as one who tempts people to sin, but rather, as one who accuses people of sin before God. His primary function, it seems from Scripture, is to accuse and condemn people based on what God has written in the minds of men and on the pages of Scripture. Why does he do this? Because Satan is the ultimate legalist. If God's throne room were a courtroom, Satan is the prosecuting attorney. It is he who brings our faults before God. He knows the law of God forward and backward and when people transgress the law, he brings accusations against them in their own minds, before other people, and to the very throne room of God. So while we often picture God as the one who accuses us of our sins and demands justice for the offenses done against Him, we must recognize that God is not the accuser of the brethren. This label applies to Satan (Rev 12:10). God is the defender of His children, and the forgiver of our sins. He does not accuse or condemn (Rom 8:1, 34-39).

Many believe that God is the one who is intent on people keeping the law, down to the tiniest detail. But as good as God's law is, He views it more as a guide, as a way to live our lives so that we can experience all the joy and fullness of life that He intends. It is not a way for Him to trip us up and catch us doing wrong. The law was given for our benefit to help us enjoy life; not to destroy our joy in life. But Satan, the destroy-er, takes the good gift of the law and uses it to ruin our joy and destroy our lives. Satan is the ultimate law-keeper. He destroys lives by defending the law, and then accuses those who break the law. He uses the law to judge, condemn, and accuse. He uses it to make us think that God is angry at us, that God is out to get us, that God does not love us, and that God does not have our best interests at heart.

When we sin, it is not God who demands that justice be served, but Satan. It is Satan who demands that the righteous requirements of the law be kept. When people do not keep God's law, Satan demands that punishment be poured out upon the disobedient as a consequence for their rebellion. Since breaking God's law brings death and destruction, when people break God's law, it is Satan who points it out and demands retribution. It is Satan who demands that "justice" be served. It is Satan, not God, who wants people to die for their sins and suffer eternal separation from God. It is Satan, not God, who demands payment for sin.

God, out of His great love, desires to freely forgive all people of all their sins, but Satan says, "You cannot! The law demands payment! The law demands death! The law demands a penalty for sin!" It is Satan who steals, kills, and destroys (John 10:10); not God! God wants the exact opposite of such things! God seeks to give, bless, restore, and heal. He wants a relationship with us. He wants fellowship with us. He wants us to be reconciled to Him, to be brought near, to tear down the dividing wall which we have erected between us (Eph 2:14). "Having defeated evil on the cross, God has put evil in a position where it cannot forever blackmail Him."[3] God forgives so that He does not have to demand justice, and in so doing, is truly just and the justifier of all.

---

[3] N. T. Wright, *Evil and the Justice of God* (Downers Grove: InterVarsity, 2006), 140.

Yes, God desires justice (Mic 6:8). He seeks justice and is delighted by it (Jer 9:24). Justice is often set against violence (cf. Isa 5:7). As such, true justice is not opposed to mercy. It is not justice *or* mercy as though they were opposed. Nor is it justice *without* mercy as if one must choose between the two. Instead, God's justice is *through* mercy and *by* mercy. He is mercifully just and justifiably merciful. God's justice is like His judgments. Though humans have twisted the concepts of both, the biblical data reveals that justice and judgment do not fall within the realm of punishment, but within the realm of setting things right and naming things for what they really are. Justice and judgment are God's *balancing* of all that has become unbalanced.

> Justice … according to Scripture [includes] loving compassion for others, taking care of the oppressed, the poor, the outcast, and even the enemy. … The nature of justice is expressed through acts of mercy.[4]

In a word, God's justice is *restorative.* He seeks to use justice to redeem, reconcile, and restore people to all that He wants for them. And how is it that restorative justice works through mercy? It works by offering free and unconditional forgiveness.

Since God is love, as the Bible teaches, then God did not need to have a debt paid or have His wrath appeased in order to forgive us. He simply needed to show us how much He loved us, that sin is not an issue with Him, and that we need not fear Him or stay separate from Him any longer. In Jesus, He showed us that He is with us in our pain and suffering, and indeed, agreed with our accusations that He was in some sense

---

[4] Sharon Baker in Jersak and Hardin, eds., *Stricken by God?*, 230.

responsible for all the evil that was going on in the world, and that He was doing something about it.

The cross does not reveal a God of wrath and vengeance who demands justice, but a God of infinite love and forgiveness. "Jesus' death on the cross was not an incomprehensible legal mistake that God had to orchestrate to satisfy the divine need for a death of a sinless person to balance the legal ledgers in heaven."[5] God forgives, not because He got paid off, but because He is love. "If God can forgive, then God can forgive!"[6] No payment is necessary.

It is the same for guilt and punishment. Is guilt really something that is transferrable? Though it is understandable in a legal setting how one person may pay the debt for someone else's crime, this does not in any way transfer the guilt from the person who committed the crime to the person who paid for it. The person who committed the crime is still guilty.

Also, how can Jesus pay for all the sins of all people throughout all time in just a few hours on the cross, or (if you believe Jesus went to hell), in just three days in the grave? Tell the young girl who is raped several times a day for 17 years that Jesus paid for the sins of those who raped her in just a few hours on the cross. There is no comfort there, let alone justice. In other words, there is no way to get rid of our guilt, other than by God simply overlooking it, ignoring it, or doing away with it, which He does through forgiveness.

Regarding punishment, is it ever just to punish one person for the sin of another? This seems more like injustice. "Even within ... [the] judicial framework it is simply not just to pun-

---

[5] Mark D. Baker in ibid., 300.
[6] Richard Rohr in ibid., 211.

ish the innocent for the sake of the guilty. There is simply no governmental or legal system in the world that would claim this."[7]

In order for God to be truly just, He extends free and unconditional forgiveness, based upon nothing but the infinite and eternal love of God. This is how true justice works, for only true and free forgiveness can "break the vicious circle [of sin] and ensure the ultimate defeat of evil."[8] This understanding of how God uses forgiveness to bring justice into the world enables us to see how God works to bring an end to the problem of violence.

---

[7] Derek Flood, *Healing the Gospel: A Radical Vision for Grace, Justice, and the Cross* (Eugene, OR: Cascade, 2012), 67.

[8] Andrew Elphinstone, *Freedom, Suffering and Love* (London: SCM Press, 1976), 80.

CHAPTER 11

REVEALS THE TRUTH ABOUT VIOLENCE

Our world is ruled and plagued by violence. It could be said that violence is both the "savior" of the world because we look to it to solve all our problems, and at the same time the destroyer of this world because violence only begets more violence. This is why one major revelation of the Non-Violent view of the atonement is in how it exposes the lie that violence can accomplish good. One of the greatest myths of all time is "the myth of redemptive violence." This myth is the primary subject of most war movies and adventure novels. The myth of redemptive violence teaches that the best way to defeat evil is to destroy it through violence. According to the myth of redemptive violence, when enemies attack, the best response is to attack back with greater force. When threats rise, we must neutralize the threat with superior firepower. This myth rules our governments, guides our relationships, and forms the foundation for our attempts at personal and family protection.[1]

The idea that violence can be used to defeat evil is nearly as old as humanity itself. From the beginning, whenever there was a problem with someone else, the best way to eliminate the problem was by killing them. We saw this with Cain, but it is also seen in blood feuds, tribal warfare, and the infinite spiral of violent revenge. Nearly everyone believes that evil can be stopped and violence can be defeated through greater violence. We believe that since "my" violence is used to stop "your" evil and violence, my violence is righteous and good and just, whereas yours is evil. But this is a myth. It is a lie. For the people who are violent toward us almost always feel that *we* are the evil aggressor, and *they* are righteous and just in their violence toward us. The way we feel about them, they feel about us. When we retaliate against them for their violence toward us, they see it as little more than another unjust and evil attack against them and attempt to respond with even greater violence toward us. This is the myth of redemptive violence: My violence is good; yours is bad; and I will use my good violence to bring your bad violence to an end. But it never works. It only and always results in greater violence.

This myth of redemptive violence was the foundational motivation behind the original murder when Cain murdered Abel, but the myth can be seen operating in all violent struggles and all wars and all blood feuds throughout history. The famous story of the Hatfields and McCoys is another example, but their

---

[1] On the topic of the Myth of Redemptive Violence, I highly recommend Walter Wink, *Engaging the Powers: Discernment and Resistance in a World of Domination* (Minneapolis: Fortress, 1992).. This is a "must read" book for all Christians.

story is duplicated millions of times throughout history and around the world, sometimes at a global level. At the beginning of the first crusade, for instance, Pope Urban II instructed the Christian crusaders to shout "*Dieu le vault! Dieu le valut! God wants it! God wants it!*" as they put their enemies to death by the sword. Even in our own country, as we marched off to war after 9/11, we sang "God Bless America" as we blew up the people we scapegoated for blowing up the Twin Towers in New York.

We are captives of the myth of redemptive violence. We feel that when we are wronged or threatened, the only proper response is to kill, threaten, or harm those who hurt us. We believe this will not only make us feel better about what was done to us, but will also stop the enemy from doing those things to us again, or to other innocent victims. But our violence toward them never stops the violence, for our enemy believes about us the same thing we believe about them, and retaliates right back.

> Violence is not the answer, but violence will persist until men rid themselves of the attitudes that justify it. As long as they remain blinded by self-righteousness, clinging to the dogmatic assumption that we-are-right-and-they-are-wrong or we-may-not-be-perfect-but-we're-better-than-they-are, so long will they justify and resort to violence.[2]

The only time that a false peace is achieved is when one of the aggressors is stronger and more powerful than the other, and is able, by brute force or threat of complete annihilation, to intimidate and frighten their foe from any further retaliation.

---

[2] Stephen Cary, *Speak Truth to Power: A Quaker Search for an Alternative to Violence* (American Friends Service Committee, 1955), 33.

But such a "peace" can only come through ongoing and ever-increasing violence toward those we view as our enemies, until we ourselves have committed more evil against our enemy in the name of "justice" than they ever committed against us. Fighting violence with violence leads only to more violence. As Jacques Ellul stated so succinctly, "Violence begets violence—*nothing else.*"[3] People often believe that violence can successfully be used to combat violence, or that there is a "right" and "just" kind of violence which can be used to defeat the "evil" sort of violence, but once again, we must face up to the fact that the difference between "right" and "wrong" violence is completely relative to the one carrying it out. Everybody, without exception, justifies their own violence. Even men like Hitler, Stalin, Mao, and Castro were able to justify and vindicate their own use of violence against others.[4] As such, violence is never the end of violence, but only its continuation. Using violence to defeat violence only exacerbates and exponentially multiplies violence.

> Pain gives birth to sin and sin to pain; aggression rallies defense and defense passes into aggression (because the best method of defense is attack). A hurts B and B hurts back. … So the hurts, injustice and angers ripple outwards, touching others as they go, in a typical vicious cycle; and evil proliferates like malignant cells in the body.[5]

---

[3] Jacques Ellul, *Violence: Reflections from a Christian Perspective* (New York: Seabury, 1969), 100.

[4] Ibid., 103.

[5] Andrew Elphinstone, *Freedom, Suffering and Love* (London: SCM Press, 1976), 78.

One of the reasons this myth of redemptive violence has ruled and dominated the world for so long, and not just the world, but Christianity as well, is because we believe that this is what God is like. We believe that God defeats violence with greater violence. Take the story of the flood as an example. In Genesis 6:5, we read that God saw how wicked and evil the world had become, and that every thought and intent of the human heart was only evil continually. What does this mean? Genesis 6:13 tells us: The whole earth was filled with violence. So here we have great evil, wickedness, and violence. And how does God respond? The text says God sent a flood to wipe out all of humanity, except eight people. This means that according to the Genesis account of the flood, God fought against violence and evil with greater violence!

This sort of behavior from God continues throughout the Old Testament. God doesn't like what is going on in Sodom and Gomorrah, so He wipes these cities out and all their inhabitants with fire and brimstone from heaven. Violence is defeated with violence. When God wants to liberate His people from slavery in Egypt, He does it through the violence of the Ten Plagues. When God wants His people to go in and remove the wicked Canaanites from the Promised Land, He tells His people to go in with sword and spear and slaughter everything that breathes. Do you see? This is the myth of redemptive violence at work in the very actions of God. We see God behave this way in the Old Testament and we think that if God can do it, so can we.

When we read the Old Testament texts as accurate descriptions of what God really said and did (rather than as accurate descriptions of what is in the heart of mankind, as proposed earlier in this book), they color our understanding of what happened on the cross. We think that just as God demanded blood and death in the Old Testament for all the wickedness and evil that was done in the world, so also, on the cross, God demanded the blood and death of His own Son as a way to appease His wrath against all the sin and evil in the world. We see the child-sacrifice of God's own Son as the ultimate act of redemptive violence. We believe that such an extreme act of violence by God reveals how serious our sin is to God.

Having fallen under the myth of redemptive violence, we believe that our great evil and violence against God could only be defeated and overcome by the greatest possible act of violence from God, which is the murder of His one and only begotten Son who was completely innocent of all wrongdoing. We think that somehow, this act of supreme violence against an innocent victim made God feel better about us and our sin. We think that somehow, God's wrath against us was quenched when He sent His Son to be tortured and killed by us on the cross. But we also think that if we do not accept what God did for us in Jesus Christ, then the wrath of God will flare back up again against us and He will cast us forever into a burning pit of flames where we will be tortured and tormented by God forever. Ultimately, the Christian doctrine about a violent hell eclipses and overcomes the six hours of violence against Jesus on the cross. According to this idea, even though God poured out His wrath against sinful humanity upon His Son, this wrath is actually only overcome when God tortures forever in burning flames those who do not accept what He did for them in Jesus. Once again, even with God, violence leads only to greater violence.

This is the greatest of all problems in the Penal Substitutionary view of the atonement. It teaches that violence can be used to solve violence. After all, according to Penal Substitution, the greatest violence of all is found in the heart of God, not just in various actions throughout history such as in the drowning of billions in the flood or the murdering of babies in the tenth plague, but also—especially!—in the crucifixion of His one and only Son. If, therefore, it is true that God engages in divine violence toward others, then it is no great leap of logic to assume that we may behave violently toward others also, especially if we can "prove" that God has sanctioned (or even ordered) such violence toward our enemies today as He has done so in the past.

The myth of redemptive violence, informed and supported as it is by a certain way of reading the Old Testament and certain portions of the New Testament, has guided our theology, our understanding of God, and our interpretation of what happened to Jesus on the cross. The myth of redemptive violence tells us that in response to our evil and violent rebellion against God, God will engage in even greater violence against us until we are all cowering in fear and submission to His omnipotent will. This violent portrayal of God has dominated western Christianity for centuries, due in large part to our acceptance of the myth of redemptive violence and how we read Scripture and understand God through the false and satanic idea that violence can be used to defeat violence.

But when we begin to build our theology and our understanding of God from the foundation of Jesus Christ and what He did and said on the cross, everything begins to change. We begin to see that God has never fallen prey to the myth of redemptive violence. We see that Jesus did not go to the cross to appease an angry God, but rather to reveal to us that God is always loving and forgiving. We see that God has never demanded sacrifice as a payment for sin, whether it was the blood of bulls and goats, or the blood of His own Son (See Appendix II for an explanation of Hebrews 9:22). We see that God does not exact vengeance, is not retaliatory, and is not violent, but is only merciful and gracious. We see that God does not maim, slaughter, destroy, or kill those who maimed, tortured, and killed Him. We humans do these things, but God does not, even though we project such behavior on Him to make ourselves feel better. All of this is what Jesus Christ reveals on the cross.

Because of the cascading revelation of God in Jesus Christ, we begin to see that something very different is going on in those violent Old Testament texts. We begin to see (as indicated in the sections above about how a Non-Violent view of the atonement informs our understanding of God, Scripture, and humans) that the violent portions of the Old Testament are not revealing God to us, but are instead revealing humanity to us, and how we blame God for our own violent tendencies. We see that out of His great love for us, God allows Himself to be condemned as a criminal and a monster, to become the scapegoat for our own sin, so that we do not annihilate ourselves or spiral down into an escalation of war and violence from which there is no return.

In Jesus Christ dying on the cross, God does not engage in violence to destroy others. Instead, He does the exact opposite in letting violence destroy Him. God does not strike back against His enemy with superior firepower. He does not call down legions of angels to overwhelm His foes and beat them back. No, when God sets out to gain victory over sin, death, and the devil, He allows sin, death, and the devil to pour out all their vengeance upon Himself. God takes it on the chin. He lets evil wear itself out by ripping Him to shreds. God does not solve the problem of evil by defeating evil with violence. Instead, He defeats evil by exposing it for what it is.

God did not kill Jesus, nor did He orchestrate the killing of Jesus. No, we killed Jesus, and in so doing, God revealed to us the fact that we are behind all killings, all murder, and all violence in the world. This is the truth about violence.

> Christ sheds his own blood to end that way of trying to mend our divisions. Jesus' death isn't necessary because God has to have innocent blood to solve the guilt equation. Redemptive violence is our equation. Jesus didn't volunteer to get into God's justice machine. God volunteered to get into ours. God used our own sin to save us. ... [The death of Jesus] exemplifies a specific kind of sin we are all implicated in and we all need saving from, and acts to overcome it. ... God was willing to be a victim of that bad thing we had made apparently good, in order to expose its nature and liberate us from it.[6]

Our killing of God in Jesus Christ, though a great crime, was also the act that exposes the sham of our man-made religious restrictions upon the infinite and unconditional love and forgiveness of God. Those religious rituals and rules were a human invention; they did not come from God. We created them out of fear, thinking that God was angry at us and these were the sorts of things that would appease His anger. The crucifixion of Jesus was one more way we sought to appease God. From our religious perspective, the things Jesus did and taught would only bring the wrath of God down upon us in full force unless we did something about Jesus. And so we did what we thought God wanted: we killed Jesus in God's name. In this way, the greatest crime of humanity unlocked revelation about the greatest love for humanity.

---

[6] S. Mark Heim, *Saved From Sacrifice: A Theology of the Cross* (Grand Rapids: Eerdmans, 2006), xi.

We have previously seen that it does no good to punish an innocent third party for the crimes of someone who sins against you. It would not be helpful to punish your son for something your neighbor did. This would be harmful to your son, would not help your neighbor see what they did wrong, and would not encourage you to forgive your neighbor. All this is true unless one condition was met. The only way you could alleviate your anger toward your neighbor by abusing your own son is to somehow convince yourself that your son is somehow responsible for the dispute between yourself and your neighbor. If you were able to pass the guilt of the dispute to your son (or some other innocent third party), only then can you hurt, abuse, or even sacrifice this innocent third party and begin feeling better about the situation with your neighbor.

Is this what God did with His Son Jesus? Some think so. In the Penal Substitutionary view, God somehow put the sins of all humanity onto the "guilt ledger" of Jesus, so that Jesus became guilty for the sins of the whole world, while we, the true sinners, received the righteousness of God in Jesus Christ. This is how verses like 2 Corinthians 5:21 are often explained.

But the truth of the cross is almost exactly the opposite. God did not need a scapegoat on which to lay the guilt for all the sins of all mankind. It is we who needed a scapegoat on which to lay our own sins. This is what we have seen repeatedly throughout this book. We are the guilty ones, and since the very first sin of the very first humans we seek to alleviate our guilt and shame by blaming others. This is what Adam did when he blamed Eve in the Garden of Eden, and what Eve did when she blamed the serpent. We do the same thing today when we blame our neighbor, boss, coworker, spouse, the opposing political party, the minority group, or the other country for the wrongs we ourselves had a hand in bringing about. Of course, nobody likes to be blamed, and so we play the blame-game, in which each party ups the ante in blaming others until eventually someone plays the trump card of the blame-game by laying responsibility for their own actions on God Himself. We do what we want to do and we justify our selfish and sinful actions by saying that "God told us" to do it, or that "God gave me no other choice." This also we see from Adam. Even though Adam blamed Eve, he actually blamed God when he says that it was God who gave the woman to him (Gen 3:12).

This explains the events of the cross. Jesus was not crucified to satisfy the wrath of God as through God demanded a blood offering to appease His anger. No, if Jesus reveals anything about God, it is that God is always loving and always forgiving. When Jesus was crucified on the cross, the one thing that is painfully obvious throughout the entire ordeal is that though the crowd blamed Jesus for numerous sins He did not commit, He was known and declared to be completely innocent of all wrongdoing. And furthermore, though the crowd justified their murderous actions by playing the "God told us to" trump card, it is obvious to all that God had nothing to do with it, but that it was the rulers and those in authority who wanted Jesus dead, and they were only blaming God for their murderous intent.

Though Jesus was not guilty of any wrongdoing, those who crucified Jesus felt threatened by His teachings or were disappointed that He had not sought to overthrow the Roman occupation, and so they wanted to see Him killed. But since they believed that murder was wrong, they had to blame others for the murder of Jesus. They did this first by trying to accuse Jesus of inciting rebellion against Rome, and when these charges did not stick they tried to incite the mob against Jesus by accusing Him of blasphemy against God. And though the ultimate verdict was that Jesus was innocent of any wrongdoing (Luke 23:4), Jesus was nevertheless crucified as a means to pacify the religious mob who claimed that God wanted Jesus to die.

So Jesus went to the cross to bear the sins of the people upon Himself. He did this, not to satisfy the wrath of God, but to reveal to humanity something that we could not and would not have ever seen in any other way. By accepting the guilty verdict and going to the cross as the innocent scapegoat, He revealed that God is never behind our violence and has never wanted scapegoats (or any other goats) of any kind. Instead, when we scapegoat others, as we scapegoated Jesus, we blame them for the wrong we ourselves have done. When we justify our violence by blaming God for what we do, we are making Him into the ultimate innocent scapegoat as we have always done since the very beginning of human history.

It is through this revelation of scapegoating violence that God revealed something greater still. He revealed that just as we scapegoated Jesus, God has always allowed us to scapegoat Him. And just as Jesus did not retaliate in violence for our violence toward Him, but forgave us, this reveals how God has always responded to our violence toward Him. He never retaliates, but always forgives.

This revelation is the real power of the crucifixion. For the cycle of retaliation and violence to end, one party must be willing to forgive. Violence is like a whirlpool that spins faster and pulls deeper with every new act of violence. When one is violent—even "righteously" violent—in response to an insult or injury, this violence leads only to more violence which threatens to drown both parties. "The only effective way to stop a whirlpool is to introduce a fixed point. A whirlpool dissipates quickly when it hits a rock that refuses to whirl."[7] Violence, even "righteous violence," is playing the enemy's game with the enemy's weapons and will never stop the downward spiral of death and destruction. The only way to stop the cycle is to stop playing the game, and the only way to stop playing the game is to forgive. This forgiveness may allow the other party to get away with murder—maybe even your own murder—but there is no other way for violence to end. We have been scape-goating God from the very beginning, and God has born it all, bearing our guilt, taking our shame, allowing us to blame Him for rape, revenge, murder, and genocide, so that, by letting us kill Jesus and forgiving us for it, He might expose our violence, thereby putting an end to violence.

> In a definitive way the cross broke the cycle of increasing aliena-tion and violence because it absorbed the worst act of violence in the world—the killing of God incarnate. God did not respond to this lashing out with a vengeful counterblow, but with forgiving love. The ultimate act of hatred was answered with the ultimate act of forgiving love.[8]

On the cross, Jesus revealed how God has always been re-sponding toward human sin and the blame we have laid upon God's shoulders for our own sin. When Jesus offers for-giveness after being unjustly accused and murdered for wrong-doing, He reveals what God has always been doing when we unjustly accuse Him for the sins we ourselves commit. We did

---

[7] Mark D. Baker references Vernard Eller who borrows the image from Soren Kierkegaard. See Brad Jersak and Michael Hardin, eds., *Stricken by God? Nonviolent Identification and the Victory of Christ* (Grand Rapids: Eerdmans, 2007), 306.

[8] Mark D. Baker in ibid., 307.

what we did out of ignorance, because we believed that our enemies were God's enemies. But God has no human enemies; His only enemy is violence, which is always and only from the devil (John 8:44; 10:10).

In this way, the myth of redemptive violence is revealed for the lie that it is. And the real way to peace is also revealed. We see that real peace does not come through war and violence, but through love and forgiveness. Seeing how God responded toward our greatest sin is the first step in learning how to live in peace with people when they sin against us. The Non-Violent atonement of God reveals the way to peace.

CHAPTER 12

REVEALS THE WAY TO PEACE

I have written a lot about the Non-Violent atonement in this book and concluded the last chapter with the exhortation to respond to violence with love and forgiveness instead of with more violence. As a result, you may be tempted to think that I am promoting pacifism. I am not. Do not think that this book is advocating a pacifistic approach to violence. It isn't. Pacifism is not the solution to violence. Jesus was not a pacifist.

The problem with the way the world (as well as Christians) approaches the issue of violence is that most people only see two options. They think we can either lash out against violence with greater violence, *or* we can refuse to resort to violence and let evil have its way. The first option simply results in more violence, while the second option does nothing to stem the violence and only creates more victims. But in Jesus Christ and how He defeated sin, death, and the devil on the cross, we now see a third way. This third way, the way of peace, is what we consider in this chapter.

The testimony of the Gospel is that only God has had the power to solve this dilemma of human bondage, the no-win choice between using violence to stem violence ... and simply joining the line of victims. It is God alone who can reveal the entire reality of the scapegoating process, reverse through resurrection its obliteration of victims, and structure an alternative option for human solidarity. This is why Christ is explicated in the New Testament as the truth, the life, and the way.[1]

One of the most startling truths about the Non-Violent view of the atonement is that on the cross, God made Himself appear guilty for crimes He did not commit. But as we have seen, since the very beginning of sin, humanity has blamed God for the things that go wrong in our lives and in this world. Adam blamed God for giving him Eve. Eve blamed the serpent which God had created. Cain blamed God for not accepting his offering of fruit. And on and on it goes.

Even today, we blame God for nearly everything. Insurance companies, though they may not actually believe God is involved, put "blame" on God for earthquakes, floods, and hurricanes by calling them "Acts of God." This tendency to blame God is due, in part, to various systems of theology that portray God as controlling every aspect and element of the universe, from the lifting of a finger and the fluttering of a butterfly wing, to the raping of little girls and the rise of nation against nation in nuclear holocaust. Individually, when bad things happen to us in life, it is not uncommon to hear someone cry out, "Why is God doing this to me?" Or, if we are a little more circumspect, we say, "Why is God allowing this to happen to me?" This second option, though slightly better, still implies that God is behind the horrible, painful, and evil things that come upon us.

---

[1] S. Mark Heim, *Saved From Sacrifice: A Theology of the Cross* (Grand Rapids: Eerdmans, 2006), 197.

Each one of us believes in the deepest part of our heart that we are victims and that God is the ultimate victimizer. He made this earth the way it is, and He placed us on this earth, and He is doing a bad job of running things. If only He would stop the rapists, the murderers, the despots, and the dictators, life would be so much better. If only He would calm the storms, quench the fires, and still the hurricanes, there would be so much less pain and suffering. In our more honest moments, we wonder what God is doing up there on His throne in heaven. Has He forgotten about us and abandoned us to our pain and misery? Or maybe, out of some sort of twisted form of divine revenge against sin, He just enjoys seeing us suffer.

It is not uncommon to hear people put the problem this way:

> If God is so good, why is His world so bad? If God is all-good, all-wise, all-loving, all-just, and all-powerful, why is there so much evil in the world? There only seems to be two options: Either God is not all-good and He somehow enjoys seeing us suffer, or God is not all-powerful and helplessly sits in heaven wringing His hands at all the pain going on in the world. A third option might be that God is simply lazy and just doesn't care about what goes on in this world.

But in Jesus, we finally see the truth, and we see what God has been doing about sin and evil since the beginning. In Jesus, we see that God fully baptizes Himself with sin. He enters fully into the condition of sinful humanity so that He appears guilty Himself. As He hung on the cross, Jesus appeared just as guilty to the average onlooker as did the two thieves on either side of Jesus. Yes, the Centurion saw something different (Luke 23:47), but most of those in the crowd believed Jesus was just as He appeared to be—a guilty criminal dying on a cross. In Jesus, God showed up, took the blame, bore the shame, and died the death of a criminal. God appeared guilty on the cross, just as God has appeared guilty of terrible acts of violence from the very beginning.

Why did God do this? Why did God make Himself appear guilty on the cross and throughout biblical history? The traditional Christian answer is "to liberate us from sin." There is nothing wrong with this answer, except that it does not explain *how* we are liberated from sin by Jesus dying on the cross. But now, through the course of this book, we are beginning to see *how*. Jesus liberates us from sin on the cross by appearing as if He Himself was a guilty criminal, even though He was not, to show us that this is what God has also been doing since the very beginning. Why? Because in so doing, we come to the realization that all the violence of God in Scripture is not actually from God, but is from us. The death of Jesus finally exposes the great lie. What lie? The lie that "God told me to do it."

In Jesus we finally see that God is not guilty; we are. We are the crucifiers. We are the murderers. We are the victimizers. We are the guilty ones. We are the genocidal warmongers.

But this still does not quite explain how this helps liberate us from sin. Here is how: The first step to breaking free from sin is to recognize that we are not only guilty for the sins we ourselves commit, but in some sense, are also guilty for the sins of others. We blame others, condemn others, accuse others, and scapegoat others. But God, in the Hebrew Scriptures, and in Jesus on the cross, steps into the place of the guilty party, and says, "I accept blame. I contributed to this mess." Sin and the violence of sin arise when we place full responsibility for sin and violence on someone else. But peace and liberty come when we, like God, take responsibility for our part in the mess of sin.

This does not mean that God actually sinned. Far from it! God cannot sin and cannot even be tempted by evil (Jas 1:13). But by stepping into the place of the guilty party throughout the Old Testament Scriptures and on the cross in Jesus Christ, God admitted and confessed that He did have some role in the way this world turned out. What role was that? He created a humanity that could sin. And so when we did sin, and when we do sin, He takes responsibility. The great truth of scriptural revelation is not that "we are sinners" but that we are sinners who blame God for our sin, and God accepted the blame for our sin so that there might be peace.

But the truth goes further still. God bore our guilt and accepted the blame for our sin so that we might do the same for others. God reveals the way to peace with Himself and peace with others by shouldering full responsibility for the situation humanity finds itself in. We can also create peace with our enemies by taking similar steps.

Peace with our enemies begins with recognizing how we have contributed to the hatred and discord. Peace begins with accepting responsibility, bearing the guilt, and shouldering the shame. This is easier said than done, but it begins with seeing ourselves as the enemy.

We cannot begin to imagine that God would love our enemies until we see that God has loved us *while we were still His enemies* (Rom 5:8-10). The beginning place of learning to love our enemies is *not* found in learning that God loves our enemies, but in learning that although we are God's enemies, He loves us. The first step toward peace with our enemies is in coming to recognize that *we are* (not *were*) God's enemies. There is still great evil in us and yet God loves us anyway. The first step in learning to create peace with our enemies is to recognize that if God set out to destroy His enemies, we are the ones who would be killed and destroyed. We are the guilty ones. We are the ones in rebellion. But God loves us and reconciles us to Himself anyway. Until we see this, we can never learn to see our enemies with God's eyes of love.

> If God were not compassionate toward us, we would be lost. And if God is compassionate toward us, with all our unredeemed evil, then God must treat our enemies the same way. As we begin to acknowledge our own inner shadow, we become more tolerant of the shadow in others. As we begin to love the enemy within, we develop the compassion we need to love the enemy without.
>
> If, however, we believe that the God who loves us hates those whom we hate, we insert an insidious doubt into our own selves. Unconsciously we know that a deity hostile toward others is potentially hostile to us as well. And we know, better than anyone, that there is plenty of cause for such hostility. If God did not send sun and rain on everyone equally, God not only would not love everyone, God would love no one.[2]

In this way, our enemy can be our surest way to finding God. "We cannot come to terms with our own shadow except through our enemy."[3] Only by allowing God to use our enemies as a mirror into our own heart do we see the enemy that resides within each of us.

As we learn to love the enemy within through the eyes of God's love for all His enemies, only then do we begin to learn love for the enemy without. Only then can steps be made toward true and lasting peace. Once we see ourselves as the ene-

---

[2] Walter Wink, *The Powers that Be: Theology for a New Millennium* (New York: Galilee, 1998), 165.

[3] Ibid., 171.

my, it is then that we begin to see how we have contributed to the anger and hostility and violence directed toward us from our enemies. We see how we are to blame. How we are responsible. How we share guilt. Once we can forgive ourselves for how we have treated those who view us as their enemy, only then can we begin to forgive them for how they have treated us.

The way to peace is through shattering the lie we tell ourselves about "the others," about "us vs. them," about how God is on our side against our enemy. We must see that we are the enemy, and that God is on the side of all. This is hard to see because it means facing the evil in ourselves, but it must be done if there is to be peace. If you are one who longs for peace, then follow the example of Jesus in being a peacemaker by taking steps to identify with your enemy by recognizing that you yourself are an enemy and bear much of the responsibility for the sin and violence in between.

When we begin to see that we are an enemy to others in the same way they are an enemy to us, we then begin to see how we have contributed to the animosity between us. Only once we see ourselves through the eyes of God and through the eyes of our enemies can we begin to accept responsibility for our part in the conflict and shoulder our part of the blame. Until we recognize this, we always and only point to the failures and mistakes of the other person, thinking that we ourselves are faultless and without blame. But when we examine our actions, words, attitudes, motives, and behaviors through the eyes of our enemies, we then see that the things for which we forgive ourselves and justify in our own minds, are exactly the same things for which they forgive themselves and justify in their own minds. By viewing ourselves and our enemies in this way, we see that we are not opposites of each other, but mirror images of each other. We are doubles, each treating the other person the way we ourselves hate to be treated.

Once we see this, we can learn to love and forgive our enemies the same way we learn to love and forgive ourselves. And this love and forgiveness for our enemies is the way that God brought peace to this world through Jesus Christ and the way that He calls us to continue spreading this peace in the world. Forgiveness, not violence, is the only way to peace.

CONCLUSION

The Non-Violent atonement is the key to everything regarding Scripture, theology, life, peace, freedom, restoration, and redemption. The Non-Violent atonement helps us understand ourselves, our history, and our motivations. Most of all, it gives us the best and clearest and most liberating picture about who God truly is. He is not a God of violence and bloodshed, but is a God who always loves and only forgives. God is love, and in Him there is no violence at all.

This God of anti-violent love is what Jesus revealed through His life, actions, and teachings, and what He revealed most clearly on the cross.[1] The God revealed in the life of Jesus is the God we are to emulate in our own life. Yet when we make

---

[1] I use the term "anti-violent" instead of "non-violent" because God is not simply non-violent. Rather, He stands opposed to violence and against violence. Non-violence implies that God could be violent, but chooses to not react with violence. Anti-violence, however, reveals that God is actively working to stop violence, and to counteract its effects. See Sharon Baker in Brad Jersak and Michael Hardin, eds., *Stricken by God? Nonviolent Identification and the Victory of Christ* (Grand Rapids: Eerdmans, 2007), 227.

God in our violent image, not only by attributing to Him our wars against our enemies, but also by blaming Him for how we killed His one and only Son (as in Penal Substitution), we end up emulating a violent god of our own making. We ignore, deny, or explain away what Jesus taught in the Sermon on the Mount, and then we go forth to do violence "in Jesus name." As a result, the house, having been swept clean, now becomes worse than it ever was before (cf. Matt 12:45; Luke 11:26).

> A violent theory of redemption legitimized punitive and violent problem solving all the way down—from the Papacy to parenting. ... If God solves problems by domination, coercion, and violent demand, then we can too. ... We ended up making God very small, and drew the Godhead into our own egoic need for retribution, judicial resolution, and punishment. Exactly what Jesus came to undo![2]

So if we are truly to follow Jesus, we must follow Him in His primary way of living. We must follow Him into peace, and specifically, self-sacrificial, non-violent peace based on a love for one's enemies and forgiveness for everything they do. This is not an easy thing to do, but following Jesus is never easy. "Healing and forgiveness have not been in the forefront of Christian history, even though it is almost the only thing Jesus does."[3] May there come a day when Christians too are known for our love.

---

[2] Richard Rohr in ibid., 210-211.

[3] Richard Rohr in ibid., 211.

APPENDICES

WHAT IS THE WRATH OF GOD?

The Non-Violent view of the atonement is one of the necessary building blocks to develop a view of God that looks like Jesus, rather than a God that looks like Thor, or worse yet, the devil. Nevertheless, people often object to the portrait of God as peace-loving, non-violent, and Christ-like, because of the numerous references in Scripture (and especially in Paul's letter to the Romans) to the wrath of God. (Other common objections include the violence of Jesus in the book of Revelation and what the Bible says about hell. Those topics will be addressed in future volumes.) So this first appendix will provide a short study on how to understand the biblical phrase "the wrath of God" in light of the crucifixion of Jesus Christ. In other words, this appendix seeks to look at how the Non-Violent atonement informs our understanding of "the wrath of God."

DOES GOD NEED ANGER MANAGEMENT?

Many people picture the wrath of God the same way we think of people who have a problem with anger. People with an anger problem let their anger build up inside until it overcomes and overwhelms them. When this happens, they lash out in violence at whoever happens to be nearby; even if it is someone they love. People view the wrath of God in a similar fashion. It is as if God tries to be merciful and forgiving, and seeks to be longsuffering and patient with people for many generations, but eventually He gets fed up with all the sin and rebellion and lashes out in anger at whichever unlucky generation of people happens to be alive at the time.

Such a portrayal of the wrath of God might be a bit of a caricature, but it is not far from how the wrath of God is typically taught. For example, this is why, we are told, God sent the flood. Over numerous generations from Adam to Noah, people became more and more sinful until God finally became so fed up with all the evil and violence, He decided to drown everybody in a great deluge. All the previous generations, whose sin "piled up" and led to the flood, were not punished but got to die of old age. It was the unlucky generation that lived during the days of Noah which received the punishment for everybody else's sin.

A similar situation occurred at the time of the Canaanite conquest. We are informed that the reason God let the Israelites languish as slaves in Egypt for 400 years is so that the Canaanites could become more and more evil. The people in the Promised Land had not yet become as sinful as was necessary for God to destroy them (Gen 15:16). So while all the generations of those 400 years grew in evil and violence, it was only the generation that was alive at the time of the conquest of Canaan that paid for their sins and the sins of their parents by getting slaughtered at the hands of the invading Israelites.

This sort of theme is also prominently displayed in the books of Judges and Kings, where entire generations live and die with each generation committing similar sins, until finally, the text says that God gets tired of all the sin and lashes out in judgment against one generation. The justification for this is that in some way or another, some biblical authors believed that children retained guilt for the sins of their parents (Exod 20:5). Of course, later biblical authors disagreed (Ezek 18:20), but that is an issue for another time. In the historical narratives of the Bible, when God can no longer contain His wrath and anger against sin, He pours it out upon one generation.

And how does God pour out His wrath? The wrath of God is usually depicted in terms of destroying sinners with floods, fire, famine, and foes. The goal of such "divine discipline" is to get future generations of people to fear God again so that they obey Him. But since some generations experience the love of God and other generations experience His wrath, God is thus depicted as a conflicted ruler who sometimes tries to rule out of fear, and other times tries to rule out of love. Lucky are the generations that happen to be alive when God rules with love, and unlucky are those who happen to be alive when He decides to lash out in angry retribution.

I completely understand that this portrayal of God has great support from a certain way of reading Scripture. I also fully admit that from one perspective, this way of reading Scripture may be "the most straightforward reading of the text." But I believe that what Jesus reveals to us about God through His life, death, and resurrection calls us to look behind the scenes of Scripture and discover the God who is truly there. And when we do this, we see that while God is covered with blood, it is not the blood of His enemies, but His own (cf. Rev 5:5-6; 19:13). When we look at God through the lens of Jesus Christ, we see that the wrath of God is not directed toward His enemies, but is accepted from them and poured out upon Him as He suffers with and for His enemies in the midst of their sin.

There are two good ways of understanding the wrath of God which do not require us to resort to a belief in an angry deity who must punish sin with indiscriminate violence against entire cultures and civilizations. The following two sections will look at these two ways of understanding wrath. Following these will be a section on how to understand wrath in the book of Romans.

THE WRATH OF GOD AS ANGUISH

The first way to understand the wrath of God is to think about it as the anguish of God. God is anguished when bad things fall upon us because we live in a sinful world. The word "wrath" in the New Testament is the Greek word *orgē,* and while it can be translated as "wrath," it also refers to anger, anguish, or indignation. The term is used frequently in the Bible to refer to human emotion about lawlessness and personal attacks, as well as God's future judgment upon sin. But the term is also used quite frequently in extra-biblical literature, especially in Greco-Roman mythology.[1] The gods of the Greco-Roman pantheon were often upset and angry about human sin and sent judgment and punishment upon the people in the form of famine, pestilence, disease, drought, and war. But is this the way the God revealed in Jesus also behaves? Is God like Jupiter, Neptune, Mars, or Pluto, who, in fits of anger, sends lighting, storms, war, and death raining down upon humanity? Or did Jesus reveal something entirely different about God? I propose the latter.

---

[1] Gerhard Kittel, ed. *Theological Dictionary of the New Testament,* 10 vols. (Grand Rapids: Eerdmans), V:386, 388.

Since "anguish" is a possible meaning for the word *orgē*, it is legitimate to think of God's *orgē* as God's anguish rather than God's anger. It is not so much that God is angry or mad against humans about their sin, but that God is deeply anguished at how sin ruins our lives and destroys everything God wants for us. The wrath of God might be described as the grief of God or the lamentation of God.[2] God does not harm or hurt us when we sin, nor does He get outraged and angry. Instead, He becomes grieved and anguished. But again, it is not the grief and anguish of a jilted lover or a rejected wife whose husband has cheated on her, but is rather the grief and anguish of a mother whose child has just become severely burned by touching a hot stove when the child was warned not to.

Would any loving mother spank or discipline a child for touching a hot stove after getting severely burned for doing so? I would hope not! The burn the child received is punishment itself! In such a situation, the mother is in anguish over the pain her young daughter is already experiencing. She is in great grief for her child. She may even cry with her child as she tries to cradle, soothe, and comfort her. If there is any anger involved at all, it is the anger of frustration at a child who refused to listen and so was hurt. This is how it is with God. If God is ever frustrated with us over our sin, it is a frustration directed at our insistence on living within the pain of sin instead of within the love and care of God.

But the wrath of God is not just God's anguish over bad things happening to His children; it is also God's warning against the bad things. It is helpful to think of the wrath of God

---

[2] Abraham J Heschel, *The Prophets: Two Volumes in One* (Peabody, MA: Prince, 1962), II:64.

in the Bible as the natural consequence of going our own way into sin. When God tells us not to do something "or else," and then we do it and the "or else" falls upon us, we tend to think that God is angry at us for disobeying Him and is punishing us for our sin. The reality, however, is that the instruction from God was not a threat of punishment at all, but was rather a warning against painful consequences.

We often make the mistake in Scripture of thinking that God's warnings are threats. That is, we think God is threatening people with punishment when in reality He is simply warning them about the natural consequences of sin. When God warns about what will happen if His people disregard His instructions, and then they disregard Him anyway and the disaster falls on them exactly as God warned, it is not God who brought the consequences of disobedience upon the people, but the people who brought the consequences of sin upon themselves by disobeying.

Consider again the image of the child burning her hand on the stove. If a mother tells her young daughter not to touch the stove or else she will get burned, the young child might think the mother is threatening her, when in reality the mother is warning her daughter of the natural (and painful) consequences of doing what should not be done. If she then touches the beautiful, glowing red coil on the stove and gets terribly burned as a result, she might even think that the pain was caused by the mother. In such situations, "the child is often hostile and sees the teacher as a tyrant or a judge."[3] If a mother warns her child against touching a hot stove but the child touches it anyway and gets burned, the child often feels fear directed at the moth-

---

[3] John V. Taylor, *The Christlike God* (London: SCM, 1992), 162.

er, for she thinks the mother caused the pain. She is, of course, quite wrong, and learns how wrong she is when her mother gathers the child up in her arms and cries with her over the searing pain in her hand.

This cause and effect of touching the hot stove is a little more obvious than many other areas of life, but the progression of events is still basically the same. When God tells us not to do something but we do it anyway and the calamity befalls us just as God said it would, we sometimes think that God lashed out in anger and brought upon us the punishment He had threatened when in fact we are only experiencing the pain He tried to warn us against.

Imagine an ancient city surrounded by walls. The walls are there for the protection of the inhabitants. Outside the walls are criminals, thieves, hungry lions, and devouring wolves. As long as the people stay within the walls they are protected. The leaders of the city may even put signs up on the gates of the walls warning people against leaving the protection of the walls. But imagine that a person wanders outside the walls. Initially, upon leaving the walls behind, a person may escape detection by the wild animals and avoid harm for a while. He may even feel an exhilarating sense of freedom and think that the warning signs at the gates had been nothing but lies. But if this person remains separated from the walls for an extended period of time, the day will come when harm falls upon him and he is attacked by wild animals. Can he at that time cry out to the walls, "Protect me!"? No, of course not! He ignored the warnings and is beyond the protection of the walls. When harm comes can he complain to the walls, "Why did you not deliver me from danger?" He cannot, for he was warned about what would happen. When harm comes as the signs on the walls predicted, can he blame the walls or the leaders of the city for causing the harm to fall upon him? No, for the harm was not caused by the warnings themselves, but by ignoring the warnings.

This is the way it works with the warnings of God. He surrounds us with guidelines and rules for our protection against the vast array of enemies seeking our death and destruction. But if we stray from the walls He has set up, we fall into wrath. It is called "the wrath of God" only because it is the natural consequences of straying from God. But the wrath of God is not the active anger of God toward sin. God is not seeking to squash sinners with His thumb or incinerate them with rays of fire. God is not like a petulant child squishing ants on the sidewalk or burning them with a magnifying glass. No, the thief comes to steal, kill, and destroy and Satan prowls about like a roaring lion seeking whom he may devour, but our God comes to love, serve, and forgive. He walks about seeking whom He may rescue and protect.

God puts gates in His walls of protection so that we may choose which kingdom we live in. We can choose to live in God's Kingdom of Light, which is full of freedom, grace, and love, or in the Kingdom of Darkness, wherein lie only death, decay, and destruction. If we choose to depart from God and live in the Kingdom of Darkness, we place ourselves in harm's way, into wrath, and if we stay there long enough, not even the long arm of God's protective hand can hold back the prowling lions forever. God "withdraws from a person or people because they have made a final decision to continue in a course of willful sin, thus depriving Him of authority to involve Himself in their affairs. God's absence leaves that person or people vulnerable to the destroyer."[4]

When a blacksmith creates a knife or a hammer, he (usually) creates it for good purposes. But in the wrong hands that same knife or hammer can cause great damage and pain. Inherent within the act of making a knife to cut vegetables for your dinner is the possibility that the sharp edge of the knife will be used to inflict pain on living beings. The knife was not created or intended to be used that way, but for a knife to be a knife it must have the sharp edge, and if it has the sharp edge it carries with it the possibility of pain. A knife is worthless if it turns to harmless rubber whenever it cuts.

This is how it works with the freedom to choose. When God gave to humanity the knife of freedom, He knew that the sharp edge of pain was inherent within that gift. If the knife was used in ways it was not intended, then the instrument of love would become an instrument of hurt. The tools given for life become tools of death when we choose to walk the path of destruction.

So the wrath of God should not be understood as "wrath from God." Wrath is not God lashing out in anger when His creatures go astray. Instead, the wrath of God is the love of God being used in wrong ways. It is the knife that God gave humanity being used to hurt rather than to heal. God made humans so they could live, love, and laugh, so they could experience joy, freedom, and relationships. But inherent within this beautiful gift is the possibility of great pain, sorrow, hate, and death. When we use God's freedom in ways He did not intend, we experience the natural consequences of using our freedom

---

[4] M. M. Campbell, *Light on the Dark Side of God* (Caldwell, ID: Truth for the Final Generation, 2003), 45.

this way; we experience the wrath of God. We experience the terrible consequences of using God's freedom in ways that God did not intend. God doesn't create or cause the pain of sinful choices to fall upon our lives any more than the maker of a knife causes the pain when a person accidentally sticks a knife in their leg. No, the painful consequences come from using a good gift in a wrong way. The wrath of God is the painful and natural consequence of using the love and freedom of God in a wrong way. It is taking the gift of a knife and rather than using it to chop vegetables for our dinner, we "test its edge" by running it along our thumb or (in some extreme cases) we slam it into our own leg. The pain that results is not God inflicting punishment upon us but is rather the natural consequences of using God's gifts in the wrong way.

Another way of saying this is that sin comes with its own punishment. When the Bible talks about wrath and the fire of judgment, it is often the self-punishment of sin that is in view. In this way, the "wrath of God" is not "God's anger toward sinful people" but is something closer to "God's righteous consequences and natural results for sin which comes upon those who act contrary to His instructions."

When we understand the wrath of God as the anguish or grief of God over His hurt children and also as the natural consequences of doing what God has warned us not to do, many of the biblical passages which talk about the wrath of God fall into focus. In fact, there is a clear progression in Scripture which shows the development of these ideas. While some of the earlier books (especially the Pentateuch) speak often and frequently of the wrath of God, the later books "attempt to loosen and even dissolve too close an association of God with wrath."[5] In one late instance, it is Satan himself who is the instrument of God's wrath (cf. 2 Sam 24:1 with 1 Chr 21:1).

Furthermore, as the concept of divine wrath developed over time, the objects of God's wrath shifted as well. While it is not uncommon in many of the earlier documents for God's wrath to be poured out upon Israel for her unfaithfulness, later documents, especially the prophetical books, describe God's wrath as a future event in which the unrighteous will perish. These later documents further describe this day of wrath as being primarily poured out upon the unbelieving and unrighteous Gentiles.[6] Even then, however, the wrath of God was rarely (if ever) described as some sort of eternal punishment after death. Instead, the consequences of the wrath of God were seen in things like sickness, persecution, enemies, premature death, or even a sense of remoteness from God.[7]

Ultimately, it can be said that God's "wrath smites the people or groups within it when they rebel against His saving will."[8] In other words, God's wrath breaks out when people refuse to live according to God's plan to rescue, protect, and deliver. God's wrath is not so much a purposeful action on the part of God, but is instead a description of what naturally happens to people when they refuse to listen to God's instructions for their well-being. Though some biblical writers call this the "wrath of God," it is really something closer to "the wrath of God's creation against those who depart from the will of God."

---

[5] Kittel, ed. *TDNT*, V:392, 396.

[6] Ibid., V:401.

[7] Ibid.

[8] Ibid., V:402.

Therefore, blaming God for the wrath of God is a bit like a child blaming his parents when he gets sick after going outside without a coat because his parents instructed him to put on a coat lest he get sick. The parents warned about the sickness but they did not cause the sickness. They simply knew what would happen if they were not obeyed, and instructed the child accordingly. The child, in refusing to obey, brought the "parental threat" down upon his own head.

Over and over again in the Bible, the wrath of God is said to be a result of how the people of God forgot Him, turned from Him, and despised His love.[9] Wrath is not, as people commonly assume, the firm and fair discipline of God upon all sinners. If it was, wrath would then be attached to His justice. But without fail in the Old Testament, the wrath of God is never attached to the justice of God. Instead, the wrath of God is linked to the failures of men and is usually written about in ways that emphasize its "irrationality, incalculability, and subjectivity."[10] There is rarely any rhyme or reason behind the wrath of God. It is impossible to measure its exercise, duration, or end, and its cause is sometimes "enwrapped in complete obscurity."[11] Since it seems unlikely for a God who is loving, merciful, just, and fair to behave in such a random, irrational, and subjective manner, this is one further reason to understand "the wrath of God" as a way of talking about the bad things that happen in this world as a result of the sinful and rebellious actions of people. Out of His great love for us, God warns us what could happen if we go our own way, and when bad things

---

[9] Ibid., V:403.

[10] Ibid., V:408.

[11] Ibid.

do happen (though they do not always occur), it is not God lashing out at us in anger or for punishment but is simply the consequence of sin falling upon us (and upon others).

The primary problem with this view of the wrath of God is that the biblical text is occasionally quite clear that when people sin, God Himself was actively sending calamity, destruction, war, bloodshed, and slavery upon His people. It is a little bit difficult, in such texts, to simply understand them as the anguish of God at how His people disregarded His warnings. So it is in these instances that the second way of understanding the wrath of God in Scripture is helpful. For this second way, we will look at the wrath of God in light of René Girard's mimetic theory.

THE WRATH OF GOD IN MIMETIC THEORY

Some texts in Scripture about the wrath of God are best understood in light of René Girard's mimetic theory. According to René Girard, since humans learn by imitating one another, this imitation often leads to rivalry between two people or groups over an object they both desire. If two children are put into a room with many toys, it is inevitable that they will both end up fighting over the same toy. Why? Because one sees the toy the other is playing with, and *mimesis,* or "imitation" rises in the second child so that he also wants that toy. When the first child sees their toy about to get taken away, the desire for the toy increases even more, and rivalry results. In larger, more adult contexts, this mimetic rivalry often leads to the death of one member or the other, or on a national level, war.

The problem, Girard points out, is that we also imitate violence. When the second child tries to take the toy from the first, the first child defends its toy by shoving the other child away.

Now feeling slighted, the second child might push back harder, or pull on the toy with more force, or maybe even hit the first child. In response, the first child might respond by biting or bashing the other child over the head with the toy. Again, among adults, these same events play out on a larger and more dangerous scale. When these things happen among extended families, corporations, or governments, mimetic rivalry leads to a rapidly expanding contagion of violence that ultimately threatens the very existence of the two societies. If left unchecked, this escalation of violence will destroy both sides of the conflict.

The only way to create peace and abort the escalation of violence is through what Girard calls the scapegoat mechanism. This is where the two warring parties agree that the *reason* they are fighting with each other is because some third-party bystander caused the struggle. This third-party bystander is an innocent outsider who had nothing to do with the initial or ongoing rivalry. Yet the two warring parties unite together and turn their wrath upon the third person or group, the scapegoat, and when they have killed this scapegoat, the two warring factions find themselves at peace with each other, thus reinforcing their belief that the one whom they killed was guilty.

Since peace was obtained through the death of an innocent third party, the two warring factions who are now at peace come to believe that the resultant peace confirms their condemnation and killing of the third party. Since peace resulted from the killing of this third party, this confirms that the third party was guilty. Furthermore, they come to believe that since this third party was guilty, and since killing this third party brought peace, God was in favor of this killing and even blessed it, because peace resulted from it.

Gregory Anderson Love aptly summarizes the Girardian perspective this way:

> Anthropologist René Girard argues that when rivalry over a limited desired object leads to escalating violence between multiple groups, the crisis of violence is surprisingly solved when a figure (or minority group) is singled out by any arbitrary mark of difference or weakness, and warring parties find commonality in attacking this one. The brutalization of the surrogate deflects attention from the previous object of desire and brings peace. The startling peace is felt as holy, and the sacrificial death of the surrogate deemed "sacred," the will of God who brought about peace through those violent means.[12]

There is much more to Girard's theory which I cannot get into here. This summary, however, is sufficient to show that Girard's Mimetic Theory helps explain many of the "wrath of God" incidents in the Bible. One defining characteristic of nearly all mimetic and scapegoating violence is that both parties (in their violence against each other *and then* in their violence against the scapegoat) claim divine sanction for their actions. Rather than saying, "I am going to hurt you because you hurt me," each party says, "God is going to hurt you because you hurt me." Of course, the instrument of God's punishment is always the person or groups themselves as they fight against or wage war upon their enemy. When the two factions unite together against the innocent third party, they *both* say that God has revealed to them that the third party is the truly guilty one and so must die.

---

[12] Gregory Anderson Love, *Love, Violence, and the Cross* (Eugene, OR: Cascade, 2010), 44.

This helps us understand much of what gets labeled as the wrath of God in the Bible. From the Girardian perspective, the wrath of God would not so much be the anger of God *Himself* against sin, but rather the way *humans interpret and understand* natural violence and their own violent behavior against others. Saying "It is the wrath of God" helps us justify our violent behavior toward others and helps us explain natural violence when it occurs. When we lash out in violence against our enemies, we justify our actions by claiming that we were instruments of divine judgment and we only act according to the will of an angry God. When we see storms and famines and wars, we believe that these things must be happening because "God is angry." In light of this, you could define "the wrath of God" as the "delusions of religion."[13]

Labelling something as "the wrath of God" occurs when we use God to justify our violence against others or explain why natural disasters occur. Wrath is religiously condemning others based on our self-righteous exclusion of others due to a false knowledge of good and evil. We think "we" are good and "they" are evil, and that God is on "our" side. Since God is with "us" and against "them," we engage in violence against "them." Similarly, when the natural disaster comes upon them we knowingly nod our heads and say God brought this upon them for their great sin. We have a little more trouble explaining natural disasters when they fall upon us, but we humans are usually able to find the "scapegoat" in our midst whose presence explains why the calamity came upon us instead of upon

---

[13] James Alison, *The Joy of Being Wrong: Original Sin Through Easter Eyes* (New York: Crossroad Publishing, 1998), 127.

our enemies. This scapegoat is then killed or expelled "in the name of God" so that future natural disasters may be averted.

Examples of this way of thinking about the wrath of God can be found in every culture throughout time. We even think and act this way today. When something bad happens to us, our first instinct is to say, "Why is God doing this to me?" Then we look for reasons in our life for why God might be angry at us to punish us in such a terrible way. When floods occur in New Orleans, when tsunamis ravage the coast of Indonesia, or when famine kills millions in Africa, we have the tendency to think that such events are the judgments of God upon these places for their sin and wicked ways. If this is the way we think today, can we not also believe that people in other cultures think this way as well, including the people who lived in biblical times? It certainly seems so.

Yet Girard's theory takes us even further into understanding the wrath of God as violence against our enemies. He shows us how a desire to imitate others leads to rivalry with them, which in turn leads to reciprocal violence. This violence, if left unchecked, results in a contagion of violence which destroys entire cultures and civilizations. The solution to this contagion of violence is the scapegoat mechanism. Warring factions are able to unite behind a common goal and come together in peace again only when they come together against a common enemy or foe (either real or manufactured). If they kill this enemy or foe, the resultant peace between those who were previously enemies proves that the scapegoat really was guilty (when they usually were not), and that the gods, who were causing the turmoil, have been appeased and are now sending peace and prosperity.

The Latin War of 340-338 BC shows how this works, as recorded by the Roman historian Livy. The Latin War took place during the time period when Italy was a collection of city-states that were at war with each other in an attempt by each to consolidate power and authority over the others. Eventually, the Roman city-state to the south found itself engaged in a battle with the Latin city-states to the north. The war began as a result of a treaty between the two sides. Livy records that while the Roman senators were calling upon the gods to bless and guard the treaty with the Latins, a Latin envoy named Annius was heard talking derisively about the Roman god Jupiter. When challenged, he stormed out of the temple, but on his way out, he slipped on the stairs, was knocked unconscious in the fall, and was killed. This was seen by the Roman senators as a sign that the Roman gods were angry with the Latins to the north and that the Latins must all be struck down, just as the gods had struck down Annius.

Many historians believe, however, that rather than Annius having died by slipping on the steps of the temple, Annius had been attacked and murdered by a mob of angry Roman senators. The story they then concocted and told was not exactly a lie from their perspective, but was simply their explanation for why they knocked Annius to the ground and killed him with blunt trauma to the head. The Roman Senators believed the gods were behind their actions and even caused them to do it, for the purpose of defending the honor or the gods. The Romans then decided that since the gods had seen fit to strike down the Latin envoy, the gods also wanted to strike down the Latin city-states to the north. And so war was declared against the Latins so that the wrath of the gods might fall upon them as it had fallen upon the envoy.

However, the early stages of this war did not go well for the Romans. They were defeated time and time again by the Latins. As the Romans tried to determine what went wrong, they decided that their numerous defeats were due to the fact that somehow, the gods were now angry with the Romans as well. In an attempt to appease the gods, they tried animal sacrifice, to no avail. So the Roman consul Publius Decius Mus "solemnly devoted himself and the hostile army to death. His figure appeared to all as more exalted than a purely human frame. He seemed to be sent from heaven as an expiation for all divine wrath, which thus fell on the enemy and destroyed them."[14] As with the death of Annius, however, many historians believe that rather than Publius Decius Mus offering himself, it is more likely that the death of Publius Decius Mus was the result of a human sacrifice to the gods. When the sacrifice "worked" and the Romans started winning their battles, the sacrificial event was transformed (as they always are) to hide the scapegoating mechanism behind sacred violence, so that the sacrificial victim became deified.[15] That is, since it was clearly the will of God for Publius Decius Mus to die, the fact that he was sacrificed was forgotten and his death was transformed into a willing self-sacrificial, divinely-sanctioned, heroic act for the good of the entire nation.

In both the death of Annius and the death of Publius Decius Mus, the "wrath" in question was actually the wrath of humans against humans which, through the exponential escalation of violence, threatened to overwhelm and destroy the entire culture. But by projecting this "wrath" upon the gods and then by using the sacred scapegoat mechanism, the violent contagion

---

[14] Kittel, ed. *TDNT*, V:391.

[15] The deaths of Annius and Publius Decius Mus fit perfectly within René Girard's explanation of mimetic desire, the scapegoat mechanism, and sacred violence. See René Girard, *The Scapegoat* (Baltimore: The John Hopkins University Press, 1986).

was averted and peace and unity were achieved, thus confirm-ing (in the minds of the participants) that the gods had been appeased. This is how "the wrath of God" works. In Greco-Roman literature, if we read between the lines of the accounts, it often appears that the wrath of the gods against other humans is often nothing more than the wrath of humans against other humans which is then credited or attributed to the gods.

So while it is helpful to think of the wrath of God as the an-guish of God over our insistence to live in sin, it is also helpful to recognize that quite often Scripture writes about things from the human perspective rather than from the divine. When, therefore, some passages talk about God's anger being un-leashed and the wrath of God pouring out retaliatory vengeance upon others, mimetic theory helps us recognize that such texts are not a revelation to us of what God is like, but are instead a revelation to us about what humanity is like and how we use God to justify our own violent tendencies toward others. This understanding of wrath is what we find when we turn to one of the books of the Bible which mentions wrath frequently: Paul's letter to the Romans.

THE WRATH OF GOD IN ROMANS

However we understand "wrath" in the Bible, it must fit with what Paul wrote about wrath in Romans. While there are nu-merous books in the Bible to which we could turn to see if the concepts about wrath we have outlined above help explain the biblical text, Paul's letter to the Romans is the premier test sub-ject for "wrath" is a key concept in Romans. Furthermore, as this letter is viewed by all as Paul's *magnum opus* on the gos-pel, a brief study of how wrath is used in Romans will help us see the relation of wrath to the gospel of Jesus Christ.

Typically, the way "wrath" is presented in evangelical circles from the book of Romans is that God is angry at people for their sin and sin requires punishment (Romans 1–3). But God loves us and so sent Jesus to die for us in our place on the cross so that we might gain the righteousness of God (Romans 4–5). However, we better be careful that we do not keep sinning or else the wrath of God might fall on us again (Romans 6–7). Some gospel presentations somewhat soften this approach by saying that while wrath may still fall upon us, wrath is not hell but is the temporal discipline of God for disobedience.[16]

This typical way of approaching wrath in Romans is based heavily on the Penal Substitution view of the atonement. Since the first part of this book has shown that Penal Substitution is not the best way of understanding the atonement, any reading of Romans which depends heavily on the Penal Substitution view is also suspect.

One indication that this is so is seen in the fact that a Penal Substitution reading of Romans sees little connection between what Paul writes in Romans 1–8 and what Paul writes in Romans 9–16. Specifically, the Penal Substitution reading of Romans has trouble explaining the transition between Romans 8 and Romans 9. The Non-Violent way of reading Romans, however, brings great continuity to the entire letter, and is therefore preferable. Nevertheless, a defense of this idea is well beyond the scope of our study here. Our present concern is only with the concept of wrath in Romans.

The first thing to consider when studying Romans is that the passages about wrath might not actually be Paul's thoughts at

---

[16] René Lopez, "Do Believers Experience the Wrath of God?" *JOTGES* (Autumn 2002): 45-66.

all, but rather the thoughts of a person who is arguing with what Paul writes. There are numerous scholars who believe that in Paul's letter to the Romans, he is using an ancient rhetorical writing strategy whereby Paul allows an imaginary objector to have his say so that Paul can refute him.[17] So, for example, when we read in Romans 1:18-32 about God's wrath against all ungodliness and unrighteousness and how people have become perverted and fallen into sin so that God must punish them with death, these words are not understood as Paul's ideas, but as the ideas of someone who disagrees with Paul. Paul quotes this objector in Romans 1:18-32 so that Paul can refute him in Romans 2:1 and following.

In this way of reading Romans, there are two gospels in Romans. There is the "gospel" of the false teacher whom Paul is dismantling point by point, and there is the gospel which Paul himself preached. The gospel of the false teacher presents a God of wrath who is angry about sin and demands blood and righteous obedience to the law for justification. The gospel which Paul preached presents a God of grace and mercy, from whom there is no condemnation, and who loves us so much that, rather than forcing us to die for Him, He came Himself to die for us.

Clearly, such a way of reading Paul is quite controversial for it takes many of the favorite Christian texts of Romans and puts them in the mouth of a false teacher. This view takes all the angry, judgmental, condemning pictures of God in Romans and assigns them to a teacher who objects to Paul's portrayal of

---

[17] Read Douglas A Campbell, *The Deliverance of God: An Apocalyptic Rereading of Justificatin in Paul* (Grand Rapids: Eerdmans, 2009). A summary can be found here: http://girardianlectionary.net/special_series/Romans1-3_read-in-light-of-Campbell.htm

a gracious and merciful God who always loves and forgives. If this way of reading Romans is correct, then there is little need to understand how the concept of wrath is defined in Romans, for most of the discussion of the wrath of God comes from the imaginary objector rather than from Paul himself.

Nevertheless, since this way of reading Romans is controversial and not widely accepted, the following discussion about the wrath of God in Romans will assume that all references to wrath come from Paul himself and are part of his personal presentation of the gospel message. In this way, we can see that even with the traditional reading of Romans the wrath of God can be explained as we have seen it defined in this Appendix.

It is important to note first of all, that most of the references in Romans about wrath do not contain the words "of God." In other words, in Romans, Paul's concept of wrath is that the wrath is not "from God" or "of God" but is an impersonal force which falls upon people due to their sin and rebellion. There is only one place in Romans where Paul writes specifically about "the wrath *of God*" (Rom 1:18), and in that instance, wrath could be understood as the natural consequences for sin as suggested above. In the one occasion where it appears that wrath is something inflicted upon people by God, Paul goes on to say that he is speaking in a merely human way (Rom 3:5). "On all the other occasions where the term appears (2:5, 8; 4:15; 5:9; 9:22; 12:19; 13:4, 5) it is impersonal."[18]

A second thing to note is that Paul contrasts the wrath of God with the righteousness of God. The two are not compatible, but are opposing ways of viewing God's way of working in the world. In Romans, Paul contrasts the righteousness of

---

[18] Alison, *Joy of Being Wrong*, 126.

God (which Paul is explaining in more detail) with the human (and incorrect) concept of the wrath of God. In other words, for Paul, believing in God's wrath is a refusal to believe in God's righteousness. If one believes that God is wrathful, one cannot believe that God is righteous.

So where does wrath come from? Again, as indicated previously, wrath occurs when we face the disastrous consequences of our own sin. It is when, despite all of God's warnings and pleadings, we jump into the fire of our own sin and get burned as a result. "Wrath is the handing over by God of us to ourselves. ... [It] is a divine nonresistance to human evil."[19] When we choose to follow ourselves instead of God, God hands us over to ourselves and we suffer the consequences. Evidence for this is found in the fact that wrath is described as God "handing over" people to their sin (Rom 1:24, 26, 28). Similarly, God "handed over" Jesus to us in the crucifixion (Rom 4:25; 8:32). So wrath "is the handing over of the Son to our killing Him that is in fact the same thing as handing us over to our own sins. Thus wrath is life in the sort of world which kills the Son of God."[20] Wrath falls upon us when God allows us the freedom to have our own way.[21]

It appears then, that the concept of wrath in Romans fits the understanding of wrath that was presented earlier. Wrath is not God's vindictive violence and anger directed toward sinful humans, but is God's willingness to let us go our own way into sin when we refuse to follow His instructions and heed His

---

[19] Ibid., 127.

[20] Ibid.

[21] Cf. Richard B. Hays, *The Moral Vision of the New Testament: Community, Cross, New Creation; A Contemporary Introduction to New Testament Ethics* (New York: Harper Collins, 1996), 385.

warnings. Yes, God is anguished when we suffer the consequences for our sin, but since sin carries its own punishment,
God cannot always protect us from the consequences of sin
without destroying the basic rules and laws of the universe He
has created. Just as God cannot change the rules of hardness
and sharpness so that we do not get cut when we run our thumb
along a sharp blade, and just as God cannot change the law of
gravity so that we do not fall when we jump off a cliff, so also,
God cannot change the laws of sin when we ignore His warnings and run headlong into greed, lust, or violence. The resultant pain we experience in such times is not pain *from God* but
is simply the pain of sin. God, in His righteousness, warns us
about wrath by instructing us to avoid sin and follow Him in
righteousness. If we ignore His warnings and refuse His ways,
we fall into sin and the resulting wrath.

Thus, the proposal about how to understand wrath in the
rest of Scripture fits well with what Paul writes about wrath in
Romans. This further supports the primary thesis above that
wrath is not God's anger toward sin, but is God's anguish
about the damage of sin, and that when God tells us what will
happen if we sin, God is not threatening us with pain and punishment, but is warning us about the damaging and destructive
consequences of sin in our lives.

THE END OF WRATH

If we take everything together that we have looked at above,
we can draw some clear conclusions about the wrath of God.
Whether we understand wrath in light of God's anguish or
wrath in light of mimetic rivalry, the one thing we can know
about the wrath of God is that God is not angry with us about
our sin.

Instead, the biblical teaching about the wrath of God is that it is we who get angry when others sin against us, and when we retaliate, we use God to justify our own sinful behavior against them. God is anguished about such behavior, for it is completely contrary to the way He wants us to live and the way He Himself lives toward us. Through biblical revelation and the unveiling of Himself in Jesus Christ, God showed us that the violence we engage in toward others is not divinely sanctioned, but is divinely blamed. God did not tell us to hate our enemies and kill them; instead we told others that God hated our enemies and wanted us to kill them—and we believed this lie ourselves, to justify our actions toward our enemies, even (especially!) when our actions toward them mirror their actions toward us.

So the gospel invites us to look into the face of our worst enemy and see a reflection of our own soul. Our enemy is not our enemy, but is our mirror image, our double, our twin. Our enemy is our prophet. We do not easily admit or accept this, however. We do not like to think that we behave toward our enemy in the same way they condemn us for behaving toward them. We prefer to think that we are morally superior, divinely motivated, and righteously justified in what we do to them.

But we are not.

Having seen ourselves in the face of our enemy, we are faced with a terrible dilemma. We must either admit that we are like our enemy, or we must kill our enemy. Since it is so distasteful to admit that our enemy is our twin, we humans most often kill our enemy. To justify our killing of them and hide the fact that in killing them we are just like them, we use God to justify our killing. And as the gospel begins to shout at us that what we are doing to our enemy is wrong, we attempt to drown out the cry of the gospel to our hearts with an escalation of violence. We seek to kill not just our enemy, but our enemy's family, relatives, and friends. We bomb, burn, and raze their town. We kill the animals and everything that has breath. And then we say that this was necessary because God willed it. We call it the wrath of God, when really it is only our own wrath toward our enemies. We use God as a scapegoat for our unrecognized violent tendencies.

> The need to override vague moral uncertainties can lead to "violent moral exaggeration," as its adherents try to suppress the growing realization that "it is all really a pack of lies." ... The weaker the sacrificial myths and rituals become, the less completely we fall under their spell and the more rapacious the mad attempt to turn violence into the "wrath of God."[22]

In the end, the unveiling of the wrath of God helps us see that the wrath is our own. Just as the Non-Violent view of the atonement ended up revealing us to us, so also, when we apply the Non-Violent atonement to the wrath of God, we end up seeing that it is not God who is angry, but ourselves. It is we who interpret bad events as God's hand of judgment, and it is we who use God to justify our own wrathful behavior toward our enemies. Only once we have seen this can we then do something about it. We must ask ourselves whether we will continue to kill our enemy in the name of God or see in our enemies the face of God. It is the latter to which the gospel calls.

---

[22] Gil Bailie, *Violence Unveiled: Humanity at the Crossroads* (New York: Crossroad, 2013), 266.

DOES FORGIVENESS REQUIRE THE SHEDDING OF BLOOD?

One of the central tenets of the Non-Violent view of the atonement is that God freely forgives people of all their sin. God did not need the death of Jesus to forgive people for their sin, for God has always been a gracious, merciful, and forgiving God, and because of these characteristics, has always been forgiving people of all their sin, no matter what. As explained in this book, the death of Jesus on the cross was not for the purpose of purchasing forgiveness from God for humanity, but was rather for the purpose of revealing that God has always been forgiving. We humans are the ones who do not forgive. It is we who demand vengeance and retribution on our enemies in the name of God. The purpose of the cross is to reconcile us to God (not God to us), and to one another. God has always been forgiving us, but the cross calls us to "forgive God" (in the sense described previously in this book), and to forgive one another, just as He has forgiven us. God does not need violence or blood to extend forgiveness, and so neither should we.

Nevertheless, one of the primary objections against the idea of an all-forgiving God who does not require blood sacrifice or violence in order to extend forgiveness is the statement in Hebrews 9:22. This verse has been used to defend the view that God demands blood sacrifice as a condition for extending the forgiveness of sins. A while back I wrote an online article providing ten reasons why Hebrews 9:22 does not teach that the shedding of blood is required for the forgiveness of sins.[1] Below is an edited and reformatted version of this article. Reading it will help you see that there are no conditions for God's forgiveness. Just as He sent His Son "while we were yet sinners," so also, He has extended forgiveness to all people for all sins "while we were yet sinners."[2]

HEBREWS 9:22 AND LEVITICUS 17:11

Hebrews 9:22 provides the main reason Christians believe that if Jesus had not shed His blood for us, we could never have been forgiven for our sins. Hebrews 9:22 quotes Leviticus 17:11 as saying this:

> … without the shedding of blood, there can be no forgiveness of sins.

From this, it appears that the case is pretty clear: The blood of Jesus is important—necessary even—for the forgiveness of sins. If the Bible says it, I believe it, and that settles it, right?

---

[1] Read the online version of this post here: https://redeeminggod.com/ hebrews-9-22-shedding-of-blood-forgiveness-of-sins/

[2] Note: This *does not* make me a universalist. There is a vast difference between having all your sins forgiven and receiving the righteousness of Jesus Christ by faith.

Apparently, God requires the shedding of blood before He can extend forgiveness.

Yet something doesn't seem quite right with that quick and tidy answer.

Just take human forgiveness as an example. We forgive people all the time without requiring that they shed blood for us. When I sin against others, I am glad that they forgive me without asking that I open a vein or kill my cat for them. So if you and I can offer forgiveness without the shedding of blood, and so can other people, what is going on with God? Is God's forgiveness of a lesser sort than ours? Or maybe His forgiveness is a more powerful type of forgiveness that requires blood? Either way, how can we reconcile verses like Hebrews 9:22 with those that says God freely forgives (Col 3:13)? Also, since when are there conditions for unconditional love, grace, mercy, and forgiveness?

Furthermore, if God's forgiveness is greater and so requires blood, then my next question is, "Why blood?" I mean, if God is the one making the rules, and sin is a serious affront to His holiness, then why did He decide that blood would appease Him? Why not require spit? Or hair? Why didn't God simply say "Without the cutting of hair, there can be no forgiveness of sins"? If God is really the one making all the rules, and He really requires some sort of payment for sin, then couldn't He have come up with something other than blood sacrifice to satisfy His demands for payment?

So maybe before we get into the question of whether or not God actually demands blood sacrifice, we must first address that question of blood itself. Why blood? The typical answer is to point to Leviticus 17:11 which says that the reason God demands blood is because "the life is in the blood." So in other words, the reason God demands blood (rather than spit or hair) is because blood costs some person or animal their life. But such an answer is not without numerous further complications. How is it right, just, or fair for God to demand that a person or animal give their lifeblood just so that He can extend forgiveness for sins, even when it is a "small" sin like a lie or a bad word? If "eye for an eye and tooth for a tooth" is true, then how can God demand "life for a lie" or "blood for a bad word"?

The reason, we are told, is that this simply reveals how serious sin is for God. While humans do not think that a lie or a bad word is that big of a deal, to God they are eternal affronts to His holy character and therefore require a significant sacrifice to cover over the eternal affront. And what more can a person give than their own lifeblood (or that of a highly valued animal)? But doesn't this make God appear to be vindictive, mean, and cruel? Isn't this portrayal of God one of the main reasons people reject God and choose not to worship Him? Most importantly of all, is not this the image of God which Jesus Himself contradicted at every turn?

Ultimately, there are so many problems surrounding the idea that God requires blood sacrifice in order to extend forgiveness, we are morally required to carefully re-examine any text which seems to indicate that blood sacrifices are a requirement or condition for divine forgiveness. Since Hebrews 9:22 is one of the key passages in this discussion, our examination will center on this crucial text. We will see that far from teaching that God desires blood, Hebrews 9:22 actually teaches the exact opposite.

The overall context of Hebrews 9 teaches that God doesn't want blood; God wants life. It is we who think that God wants blood, and we get this idea from pagan religions. Jesus went to the cross, not to reinforce and support the idea that God wants blood sacrifice, but to expose and redeem it. Below are ten reasons why Hebrews 9:22 does not teach that God requires blood for the forgiveness of sins.

1. HEBREWS 9:22 CONTRASTS JESUS WITH MOSES

The first thing to notice about the context of Hebrews 9:22 is that the author is clearly contrasting the sacrificial system of the Mosaic Law with what Jesus accomplished in His death on the cross.

One way to note this is by looking back to Hebrews 9:15, which is the opening statement in the larger context of this discussion about sacrifice and blood. In Hebrews 9:15, the author writes about the "redemption of the transgressions." The word used here is not the normal word for "sin" in the New Testament, but is *parabainō,* and means to overstep or go beyond the boundaries. The *TDNT* says that *parabainō* is closely connected with sin in the New Testament, but primarily in the sense of using human tradition to disobey the law of God while claiming to be the fulfillment of the law.

In other words, *parabainō* takes place when someone tries to explain and apply the law of God, but actually ends up doing the exact opposite of what the law says. The author of Hebrews indicates that Jesus came to redeem sin, that is, to redeem the *parabainō* type of sin. More specifically still, Jesus came to redeem the sin of misusing the law. It is this issue that concerns the author of Hebrews in the context of Hebrews 9 (and possibly the letter as a whole).

2. HEBREWS 9:22 SAYS THERE IS PURIFICATION AND FORGIVENESS WITHOUT BLOOD

Second, it is important to note that even in Hebrews 9:22, the author adamantly states that there is purification and forgiveness apart from the shedding of blood. The author says, "almost all things are purified with blood ..." In other words, there are some things that are purified without blood. This fits with what the Levitical law teaches.

Under the Levitical law, purification and forgiveness was extended under a variety of circumstances, including the washing with water (Lev 15:16-17; 17:15), anointing with oil (Lev 14:29), burning flour (Lev 5:11-13), giving money (Exod 30:11-16), or releasing an animal into the wild (Lev 16:10). In fact, when it comes to intentional sins, there was no offering of any kind which was prescribed by the law. All the sacrifices and offerings of the law are for unintentional sins only. When an Israelite sinned intentionally (as they most certainly did, just as we do), the only way they could receive forgiveness from God was to look to Him for it in faith, depending solely on His grace to extend forgiveness freely (just like us)!

The author of Hebrews knows all this, which is why he says that *almost* all things are purified by blood. There are some things which are *not* purified by blood, which means that blood was not required under all circumstances.

3. HEBREWS 9:22 IS NOT ABOUT SIN; BUT ABOUT THE COVENANT

Nevertheless, it is not exactly true that *almost all* things required blood for purification. A quick reading of the Levitical law reveals that *most things did not require blood*.

So what does the author of Hebrews mean? The context indicates that the author specifically has in mind the tabernacle and the religious items within the tabernacle (Heb 9:21). The author is talking about the initial dedication ceremony of the first tabernacle built by Moses. This purification and dedication ceremony initiated the Mosaic Covenant (Heb 9:18-19). While it is true that *almost all things* in the tabernacle purification ceremony required blood for purification, it is not true that almost all other things required blood for purification. Most things did not require blood.

So the author of Hebrews is not giving a general principle in Hebrews 9:22 for how people receive forgiveness of sins, but is instead referring to how the covenant of Moses was initiated by blood.

4. HEBREWS 9:22 SAYS THAT SHEDDING OF BLOOD CAME FROM THE LAW

Fourth, notice that the author of Hebrews specifically states where the instruction about offerings of blood came from. He does not say, "and God commanded that all things be purified with blood, for without the shedding of blood there is no forgiveness of sins." No, Hebrews 9:22 specifically states that these things are "according to the law." This is different than saying that this is according to what God wanted.

Of course, those of us who hold to the inspiration and inerrancy of Scripture don't see much difference between something the law stated and something God stated, and yet we must be careful because numerous Old Testament prophets emphatically declared that God is not the one who gave the law or commanded that the people offer sacrifices. These biblical prophets taught that God was not pleased with these sorts of religious rituals, nor did He ever want them (cf. Jer 7:21-23; Amos 5:21-24; Micah 6:6-8).

So while we believe in the inspiration and inerrancy of Scripture, the Scripture does not seem to speak with a unified voice about the origin of the sacrificial system. It appears from later prophets that the sacrifices of the law were not what God wanted. Interestingly, this is the same point the author of Hebrews makes in 10:5-6. We must be careful about equating what the law says about sacrifices, with what God *actually* wanted when later prophets claim that God did not want or command that sacrifices be carried out.

Regardless of how we understand this thorny issue, most agree that in Hebrews 9:22 the author is simply contrasting how the law inaugurated the Mosaic Covenant with how Jesus inaugurated the New Covenant.

5. THE SHEDDING OF BLOOD NEVER BROUGHT FORGIVENESS!

In light of this contrast between the two covenants, notice that the author of Hebrews deftly shows how the Mosaic Covenant, with all its bloody sacrifices, was never able to accomplish what it promised. The author of Hebrews points out that it is "impossible for the blood of bulls and goats to take away sins" (Heb 10:4).

Though it was the law that promised the forgiveness of sins through blood sacrifices, the simple fact that the law required perpetual sacrifices revealed that the law could not deliver what it promised. Nobody was ever actually forgiven through the blood of a sacrifice. So according to the author of Hebrews, though the law required blood for forgiveness, blood didn't provide any forgiveness. The law didn't work. The blood sacrifices never achieved forgiveness for anyone.

Jesus was already preaching forgiveness of sins and forgiving sins before he died. He did not have to wait until after the resurrection to do that. Blood is not acceptable to God as a means of uniting human community or a price for God's favor.[3]

6. HEBREWS 9:22 IS NOT ABOUT FORGIVENESS OF SINS

This leads to a sixth point about Hebrews 9:22 which should not be missed. I intentionally misquoted Hebrews 9:22 at the beginning of this appendix. I quoted Hebrews 9:22 as saying that "without the shedding of blood there is no forgiveness of sins." But Hebrews 9:22 does not include those final two words, "of sins." Hebrews 9:22 says nothing about sin at all. Yes, sin is mentioned in Hebrews 9:26-28, but only in reference to the sacrifice of Jesus. The first time the author references sin in connection to the sacrificial blood of the Mosaic Covenant is in Hebrews 10:4, where, as we have just seen, the only connection between sin and blood is that sin cannot be taken away by the blood of bulls and goats.

So what is the blood for in Hebrews 9:22? Again, as we saw above, it was for the purification of the tabernacle and its vessels when Moses inaugurated the first covenant. Modern western Christians are so infatuated with sin, that we see sin everywhere. We believe that our biggest problem in the world is sin

---

[3] S. Mark Heim, *Saved From Sacrifice: A Theology of the Cross* (Grand Rapids: Eerdmans, 2006), xi.

and that God is sitting in heaven trying to figure out how to stop us all from sinning.

I believe, however, that God is not nearly as concerned with sin as we are. Before the majesty of God's holiness and love, all the sin of the world is little more than an annoying flea jumping around on the ground by his foot. Sin is not that big of a deal for God. The only reason He is concerned at all about sin is because sin hurts and damages us. Since God loves us beyond all imagination, He wants to do something about the flea of sin because it has bitten us and injected us with all sorts of harmful toxins. Also, God must do something about sin because sin is a big deal for Satan, and Satan uses sin to lay claim to our lives, which is something God does not want. But this too is another rabbit trail which we must avoid for now. The bottom line is that sin is not a big deal for God, and sin is not the issue in Hebrews 9:22, nor is it even mentioned.

7. HEBREW 9:22 ISN'T EVEN ABOUT "FORGIVENESS"

But what about the word "forgiveness" in Hebrews 9:22? Doesn't the word "forgiveness" indicate that sin is the issue? No, it does not.

The word which the author uses here is the Greek word *aphesis*. As we saw earlier in this book, this word does not mean "forgiveness" in the way that modern, English-speaking people think about forgiveness. Instead, *aphesis* is something closer to "deliverance" or "release." It has in mind the picture of someone who is enslaved or in chains, but then is liberated, unchained, or set free.

In Scripture, we are freely forgiven of all our sins, past, present, and future. This forgiveness is granted to us completely and only by the grace of God. We are, however, called upon to obey God so that we might enjoy the freedom from sin that He wants for us. Sin injects us with toxins that further enslave us, which God wants to liberate us from. This sort of release often requires something on the part of the one who is being released, lest they fall right back into slavery after having been released. In this way, *aphesis* is a symbiotic forgiveness. It not only requires that the liberator unlock the chains; it also requires that the liberated run away from what chained them in the first place so that they remain free.

This means that the "forgiveness" of Hebrews 9:22 is not about the forgiveness of sins we receive from God which He grants freely to everybody by His grace, but is about how to live a life that is not enslaved and in bondage to the addiction of sin. The word *aphesis* tells us that Hebrews 9:22 is about freedom from sin and being released from slavery and captivity to sin. But there is something more to learn from the way the word *aphesis* is used in this verse, as the next point reveals.

8. THE "RELEASE" OF HEBREWS 9:22 IS A RELEASE OF THE COVENANT

Usually, *aphesis* refers to the release of people from slavery and bondage. In Hebrews 9, however, it is not *people* who are being released, but the covenant itself. The blood of Hebrews 9:22 has absolutely nothing to do with the removal of sin. Instead, the blood was for the enactment of the Mosaic Covenant. The author of Hebrews could not be clearer. He says that a testament, or will, is not put into effect until the one who wrote it dies (Heb 9:16-17). My wife and I have Wills, and as is the case with all Wills, they do not go into effect until we die. A "Last Will and Testament" has no power while we live.

So after Moses wrote the covenant, or the testament, he enacted a death over it to make it effective and active upon the people (Heb 9:19-21). So the "Last Will and Testament" which is the Mosaic Covenant is in force. The question then becomes, "Whose Last Will and Testament was this?" In killing an animal to symbolize a death so that the Will could go into effect, who was it that symbolically died? The answer is that it was God. The covenant, or Will, was God's covenant to the people. But since God Himself could not come down to die and so enact the covenant, Moses symbolized the death of God with "the blood of calves and goats, with water, scarlet wool, and hyssop" (Heb 9:19).

The "release" in Hebrews 9:22 then, is the release of the covenant. Prior to the shedding of the blood of the bulls and goats, the covenant was not active. It was under lock and key. A death was needed to free it, liberate it, or enact it. And since God was the "testator" (Heb 9:16), but God could not die, Moses killed calves and goats to symbolize the death of God, and in so doing, enacted the covenant of God with His people, Israel.

Again, we see that Hebrews 9:22 has nothing whatsoever to do with sin. Nor does Hebrews 9:22 have anything to do with the conditions of forgiveness, for as we have seen above, the covenant offered numerous ways for people to receive purification from sin, and when it came to forgiveness for intentional sins, the Israelites believed on the grace of God for forgiveness just as we do.

9. THE PEOPLE WERE ALSO RELEASED FROM SLAVERY

But the "remission" or "release" of Hebrews 9:22 is not just the release or enactment of the covenant. The implementation of the first covenant with Moses took place after the Israelite people had been delivered and redeemed from captivity in Egypt. From a purely legal standpoint, they were runaway slaves. According to the laws of slavery, as long as a slave is still living and has not yet been set free, the slave is still a slave, even if they run away. So the redemption enacted as part of the Mosaic Covenant was the redemption of the slaves from slavery in Egypt. The death of the calves and goats not only symbolized the death of God to enact the covenant, but also symbolized the death of the Israelite people to their former life of slavery in Egypt. This is partly why the blood was sprinkled on them as well. They were sprinkled with blood to symbolize their death, and therefore, their liberation from slavery.

Through the Mosaic Covenant, the people of Israel died to their old identification as slaves to the household of Pharaoh (i.e., Egypt), and were raised again to a new identification as members of the household of God. This occurred when the water and the blood was sprinkled not just on the book of the covenant, but also on all the people (Heb 9:19). They were dying to their past and were being born again into a new family. As members of this new family, they had new household rules to live by, which were enumerated in the Mosaic Covenant.

10. HEBREWS 9:22 IN THE CONTEXT OF HEBREWS 9–10

All of this together helps us understand the discussion in Hebrews 10 that follows about how the New Covenant, which was enacted through the death of Jesus, is far superior in all ways to the Old Covenant which was enacted through the blood of animals. This also helps explain why Hebrews 10 talks about sin so much. Though we have seen that Hebrews 9:22 is not talking about the forgiveness of sins, we often get confused about the rest of Hebrews 9 and on into Hebrews 10 because there are many references to the sacrifice or offerings of Jesus Christ for our sins.

The best way to understand this is to remember what we have learned from Hebrews 9:16-22 about why the blood of the calves and goats was sprinkled over the tabernacle and its instruments, along with the book of the covenant and the people, on the day the Mosaic Covenant was instituted among them. The blood was to inaugurate the covenant and indicate to the people that they had been set free from slavery.

All of this is exactly the same with the death of Jesus. Jesus did not die to rescue us from the wrath of God. Nor did Jesus die to secure for us the forgiveness of sins. God has always freely forgiven people of their sins. The death of Jesus on the cross, therefore, was to inaugurate the New Covenant of God with the entire world, and to indicate to all people that we were no longer slaves to sin. That second point is critical. Jesus did not die *for God* because of sin. Jesus died for sin. God's holiness did not demand that Jesus be put to death. No, it was the devil that demanded death and blood (cf. Heb 2:14-15). Sin was the certificate of ownership which the devil held over the heads of humanity. By dying, Jesus cancelled this debt of sin so that the devil could no longer have any claim upon us. This happened because just as all sinned in Adam, and so became slaves to death and the devil, so all died and were raised to new life in Jesus, and so were liberated and redeemed from our slavery to death and the devil (cf. Rom 5:12-21). Just as the Israelites in the wilderness died to Pharaoh through the sacrifice and were raised to new life as the people of God, so also, all people in Jesus died to sin, death, and devil, and were raised to new life in the family of God. This is the basic meaning of the discussion in Hebrews 10 about the sacrifice of Jesus for sin. But the discussion in Hebrews 9–10 goes beyond this as well. The author of Hebrews intentionally subverts the sacrificial elements of the Mosaic Covenant by transitioning away from images of blood and death, and writing instead about offerings and purification. Let us note just a few of these instances.

Following immediately after Hebrews 9:22, we read that Jesus also purified the heavenly sanctuary. And just as the first ceremony indicated the inauguration of the Mosaic Covenant and the death of the people to their past enslavement to Egypt, so also, the actions of Jesus indicated the inauguration of the New Covenant and the death of the people to their enslavement to sin.

In Hebrews 10:1-4, the author emphasizes the complete failure of the Mosaic Law to do anything about sin. In Hebrews 10:2, we are informed that if the law could have taken away sin, the people would have stopped making sacrifices, for they would have had no more consciousness of sins. Yet the sacrifices themselves are a reminder of sins, even though they do nothing about the sins. This is why the law failed regarding sin.

So was the Law a failure? No. In Hebrews 10:5-10, the author indicates that the sacrificial system was never intended to take away sins and that God Himself never wanted such sacrifices or took any pleasure in them. Again, God is a God of life; not death. What God did want, however, was a life lived in obedience to the will of God, which is exactly the "offering" which Jesus brought. This understanding of "offering" and "sacrifice" as the life of Jesus rather than the death of Jesus is critical for the rest of the chapter (and completely in line with Rom 12:1-2, where God wants a living sacrifice, not a dead one). While it is true that Jesus died a bloody and gruesome death on the cross, it is critical to recognize that the death of Jesus on the cross was for sin, while the life of Jesus was for God. God did not want nor desire the death of Jesus. God always and only wants life. Jesus died to reveal our sin to us, not so that God might forgive our sin.

> This is the disclosure of the Cross: vengeance is human violence that finally breaks against God. ... The point of the Cross is ... that our minds might be renewed by the disclosure and we might take rational responsibility for our violence.[4]

The law also was intended to reveal our sin, but all it ended up doing was amplifying it.

Building upon this truth, Hebrews 10:11-18 moves on to compare and contrast the covenant enacted by Moses and the covenant enacted by Jesus Christ. After explaining that the sacrifices and offerings of the priests could never do anything about sin, Hebrews 10:12-13 shows that Jesus not only dealt with sin once and for all through His death, but actually perfected forever those who are in Him. The author then makes the absolutely shocking statement that God (and Moses) knew from the very beginning that the Law of Moses was obsolete and useless for doing anything permanent about sin. The author of Hebrews points at what the Holy Spirit said through the prophet Jeremiah about the new covenant (Jer 31:33-34) and then ties this together with the word "remission" (*aphesis*) which was used in Hebrews 9:22. In so doing, the author indicates the truth that Moses knew from the very beginning that

---

[4] Robert G. Hamerton-Kelly, *Sacred Violence: Paul's Hermeneutic of the Cross* (Minneapolis: Fortress, 1992), 153.

his law was temporary, obsolete, and ineffective for doing anything about sin.

In Exodus 20, after God had given the Ten Commandments, God wanted to speak to the people of Israel Himself. But they were too scared of God, and declared that they would rather have Moses to speak to God for them (Exod 20:19). What follows in Exodus 21 through most of the rest of the Pentateuch is called "the Mosaic Law" for good reason. It was how Moses believed God wanted the people of Israel to live out the Ten Commandments. But forty years later, Moses saw that what he had given to the people was a complete failure. He had been with them for forty years (Deut 29:5) and knew that the law would be completely ineffective in helping them follow God and live rightly (cf. Deut 31:16-21). As a result, Moses knew that what he had given to the people would be replaced by what God had wanted all along, namely, a personal relationship with each person. Before Moses died, he prophesied that his law would pass away and would be replaced with the law of God written upon men's hearts (Deut 30:6-20). Long before Jeremiah ever prophesied that God would do away with the written law and write His law upon our hearts and minds, Moses had said the same thing (cf. Deut 30:6, 14). Paul understood Deuteronomy 30 in this way as well (cf. Rom 10:7-8). In a recent book on the Pentateuch, John Sailhammer has argued that one of the central points of the Pentateuch is to show that the law was ineffective, obsolete, and not at all what God had wanted for His people.[5] Instead, God wanted faith, humility, mercy,

---

[5] John H. Sailhammer, *The Meaning of the Pentateuch: Revelation, Composition, and Interpretation* (Downers Grove, IL: IVP, 2009).

and righteousness, which are the things the law could not provide.

Jesus provided what the law could not, which brings us back to Hebrews 10. Jesus lived the way God intended for humans, and in so doing accomplished several things. First, Jesus crucified the law of sin and death (Heb 9:26-28). Second, Jesus revealed what God had always wanted for His people (Heb 10:16-17). Third, Jesus revealed how God's people could live for love and life instead of sin and death (Heb 10:20-23). In Jesus, we learn that God no longer wants death, and He never did. God always and only wants life.

CONCLUSION

These ten points provide clear evidence that Hebrews 9:22 is not teaching that God requires blood sacrifice for the forgiveness of sins. Instead, the context of Hebrews 9:22 reveals the exact opposite, and also reveals some deep and amazing truths about the grace of God in our lives. In this text, we learn that God always forgives sins freely and that He does not need or want blood, but instead wants us to live life in the freedom for which we have been set free. Jesus Christ is victorious and we are the recipients of His triumph.

SUGGESTED BIBLIOGRAPHY

To learn more about many of the concepts introduced by this book, start by reading the following books.

Cross Vision, by Gregory A. Boyd
The Crucifixion of the Warrior God, by Gregory A. Boyd
Sinners in the Hands of a Loving God, by Brian Zahnd
The Crucified God, by Jürgen Moltmann
The Crucifixion, by Fleming Rutledge
Mimetic Theory and Biblical Interpretation, by Michael Hardin
Christus Victor, by Gustaf Aulen
Four Views on the Atonement, ed. by Beilby and Eddy
The Christ-like God, by John Taylor
The Non-Violent Atonement, by J. Denny Weaver
A More Christlike God, by Brad Jersak
Violence Unveiled, by Gil Bailie
Saved from Sacrifice, by S. Mark Heim
Executing God, by Sharon Baker

ABOUT J. D. MYERS

J. D. Myers is an author, blogger, and teacher. Much of his content can be found at RedeemingGod.com, where he seeks to help liberate people from the shackles of religion. He lives in Oregon with his wife and three beautiful daughters.

If you appreciated the content of this book, would you consider recommending it to your friends and leaving a review on Amazon? Thanks!

JOIN JEREMY MYERS AND LEARN MORE

Take Bible and theology courses by joining Jeremy at
RedeemingGod.com/join/

Receive updates about free books, discounted books, and new books by joining Jeremy at
RedeemingGod.com/read-books/

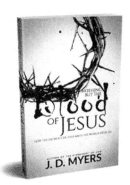

Nothing but the Blood of Jesus: How the Sacrifice of Jesus Saves the World from Sin

Do you have difficulties reconciling God's behavior in the Old Testament with that of Jesus in the New?

Do you find yourself trying to rationalize God's violent demeanor in the Bible to unbelievers or even to yourself?

Does it seem disconcerting that God tells us not to kill others but He then takes part in some of the bloodiest wars and vindictive genocides in history?

The answer to all such questions is found in Jesus on the cross. By focusing your eyes on Jesus Christ and Him crucified, you come to understand that God was never angry at human sinners, and that no blood sacrifice was ever needed to purchase God's love, forgiveness, grace, and mercy.

In *Nothing but the Blood of Jesus*, J. D. Myers shows how the death of Jesus on the cross reveals the truth about the five concepts of sin, law, sacrifice, scapegoating, and bloodshed. After carefully defining each, this book shows how these definitions provide clarity on numerous biblical texts.

Building on his previous book, 'The Atonement of God', the work of René Girard and a solid grounding in the Scriptures, Jeremy Myers shares fresh and challenging insights with us about sin, law, sacrifice, scapegoating and blood. This book reveals to us how truly precious the blood of Jesus is and the way of escaping the cycle of blame, rivalry, scapegoating, sacrifice and violence that has plagued humanity since the time of Cain and Abel. 'Nothing but the Blood of Jesus' is an important and timely literary contribution to a world desperately in need of the non-violent message of Jesus. –Wesley Rostoll

So grateful to able to read such a profound insight into the Bible, and the truths it reveals, in this new book by Jeremy Myers. When reading both this book and the Atonement of God, I couldn't help but feel like the two disciples that walked with Jesus after His resurrection, scripture says that their eyes were opened...they knew Him... and they said to one another, 'Did not our heart burn within us while He talked with us on the road, and while He opened the Scriptures to us?'

My heart was so filled with joy while reading this book. Jeremy you've reminded me once more that as you walk with Jesus and spend time in His presence, He talks to you and reveals Himself through the Scriptures. –Amazon Reader

Purchase the eBook for $8.99
Purchase the Paperback for $14.99

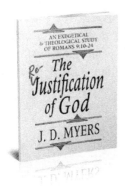

The Re-Justification of God:
A Study of Romans 9:10-24

Romans 9 has been a theological battleground for centuries. Scholars from all perspectives have debated whether Paul is teaching corporate or individual election, whether or not God truly hates Esau, and how to understand the hardening of Pharaoh's heart. Both sides have accused the other of misrepresenting God.

In this book, J. D. Myers presents a mediating position. Gleaning from both Calvinistic and Arminian insights into Romans 9, J. D. Myers presents a beautiful portrait of God as described by the pen of the Apostle Paul.

Here is a way to read Romans 9 which allows God to remain sovereign and free, but also allows our theology to avoid the deterministic tendencies which have entrapped certain systems of the past.

Read this book and—maybe for the first time—learn to see God the way Paul saw Him.

Reviews from Amazon

Fantastic read! Jeremy Myers has a gift for seeing things from outside of the box and making it easy to understand for the rest of us. The Re -Justification of God provides a fresh and insightful look into Romans 9:10-24 by interpreting it within the context of chapters 9-11 and then fitting it into the framework of Paul's entire epistle as well. Jeremy manages to provide a solid theological exegesis on a widely misunderstood portion of scripture without it sounding to academic. Most importantly, it provides us with a better view and understanding of who God is. If I had a list of ten books that I thought every Christian should read, this one would be on the list. –Wesley Rostoll

I feel the author has spiritual insight to scripture and helps to explain things. I would recommend any of his work! –Uriah Scott

Purchase the eBook for $2.99

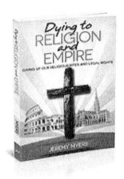

Dying to Religion and Empire

Could Christianity exist without religious rites or legal rights? In *Dying to Religion and Empire*, I not only answer this question with an emphatic "Yes!" but argue that if the church is going to thrive in the coming decades, we must give up our religious rites and legal rights.

Regarding religious rites, I call upon the church to abandon the quasi-magical traditions of water baptism and the Lord's Supper and transform or redeem these practices so that they reflect the symbolic meaning and intent which they had in New Testament times.

Furthermore, the church has become far too dependent upon certain legal rights for our continued existence. Ideas such as the right to life, liberty, and the pursuit of happiness are not conducive to living as the people of God who are called to follow Jesus into servanthood and death. Also, reliance upon the freedom of speech, the freedom of assembly, and other such freedoms as established by the Bill of Rights have made the church a servant of the state rather than a servant of God and the gospel. Such freedoms must be forsaken if we are going to live within the rule and reign of God on earth.

This book not only challenges religious and political liberals but conservatives as well. It is a call to leave behind the comfortable religion we know, and follow Jesus into the uncertain and wild ways of radical discipleship. To rise and live in the reality of God's Kingdom, we must first die to religion and empire.

Reviews from Amazon

Jeremy is one of the freshest, freest authors out there— and you need to hear what he has to say. This book is startling and new in thought and conclusion. Are the "sacraments" inviolate? Why? Do you worship at a secular altar? Conservative? Liberal? Be prepared to open your eyes. Mr. Myers will not let you keep sleeping!

This book is tight, well-written, and WELL worth the price. As a subscriber, I received an early free copy, but I am buying a copy today because this book is that good, I want to have it handy to re-read, annotate and write commentary upon.

For all free-thinkers, for all who consider themselves "spiritual," for all who have come out or are on the way out of "Babylon," this is a new book for you! Treat yourself, buy this book and enjoy it! –Shawn P. Smith

Jeremy Myers is one or the most thought provoking authors that I read, this book has really helped me to look outside the box and start thinking how can I make more sense of my relationship with Christ and how can I show others in a way that impacts them the way that Jesus' disciples impacted their world. Great book, great author. –Brett Hotchkiss

Purchase the eBook for $6.99
Purchase the Paperback for $9.99

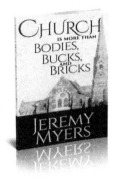

Church is More than Bodies, Bucks, & Bricks

Many people define church as a place and time where people gather, a way for ministry money to be given and spent, and a building in which people regularly meet on Sunday mornings.

In this book, author and blogger Jeremy Myers shows that church is more than bodies, bucks, and bricks.

Church is the people of God who follow Jesus into the world, and we can be the church no matter how many people we are with, no matter the size of our church budget, and regardless of whether we have a church building or not.

By abandoning our emphasis on more people, bigger budgets, and newer buildings, we may actually liberate the church to better follow Jesus into the world.

Reviews from Amazon

This book does more than just identify issues that have been bothering me about church as we know it, but it goes into history and explains how we got here. In this way it is similar to Viola's Pagan Christianity, but I found it a much more enjoyable read. Jeremy goes into more detail on the three issues he covers as well as giving a lot of practical advice on how to remedy these situations. –Porten2

This book surprised me. I have never read anything from this author previously. The chapters on the evolution of the tithe were eye openers. This is something that has bothered me for years in the ministry. It may be truth that is too expensive to believe when it comes to feeding the monster. –Karl Ingersoll

Since I returned from Africa 20 years ago I have struggled with going to church back in the States. This book helped me not feel guilty and has helped me process this struggle. It is challenging and overflows with practical suggestions. He loves the church despite its imperfections and suggests ways to break the bondage we so often find ourselves in. –Truealian

Jeremy Meyers always writes a challenging book ... It seems the American church (as a whole) is very comfortable with the way things are ... The challenge is to get out of the brick and mortar buildings and stagnant programs and minister to the needy in person with funds in hand to meet their needs especially to the widows and orphans as we are directed in the scriptures. – GGTexas

Purchase the eBook for $7.99
Purchase the Paperback for $9.99

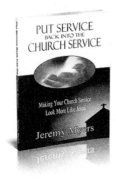

Put Service Back Into the Church Service

Churches around the world are trying to revitalize their church services. There is almost nothing they will not try. Some embark on multi-million dollar building campaigns while others sell their buildings to plant home churches. Some hire celebrity pastors to attract crowds of people, while others hire no clergy so that there can be open sharing in the service.

Yet despite everything churches have tried, few focus much time, money, or energy on the one thing that churches are supposed to be doing: loving and serving others like Jesus.

Put Service Back into the Church Service challenges readers to follow a few simple principles and put a few ideas into practice which will help churches of all types and sizes make serving others the primary emphasis of a church service.

Reviews from Amazon

Jeremy challenges church addicts, those addicted to an unending parade of church buildings, church services, Bible studies, church programs and more to follow Jesus into our communities, communities filled with lonely, hurting people and BE the church, loving the people in our world with the love of Jesus. Do we need another training program, another seminar, another church building, a remodeled church building, more staff, updated music, or does our world need us, the followers of Jesus, to

BE the church in the world? The book is well-written, challenging and a book that really can make a difference not only in our churches, but also and especially in our neighborhoods and communities. –Charles Epworth

Do you ever have an unexplained frustration with your church, its service or programs? Do you ever feel like you are "spinning your wheels" when it comes to reaching others for Christ? This book helps to explain why this might be happening, and presents a convincing argument for why today's church services are mostly ineffective and inefficient. You will read concepts explained that you've not fully heard before. And you will get hints as to how it could, or should, work. –MikeM

Purchase the eBook for $5.99
Purchase the Paperback for $5.99

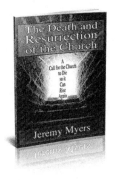

The Death and Resurrection of the Church

In a day when many are looking for ways to revitalize the church, Jeremy Myers argues that the church should die.

This is not only because of the universal principle that death precedes resurrection, but also because the church has adopted certain Satanic values and goals and the only way to break free from our enslavement to these values is to die.

But death will not be the end of the church, just as death was not the end of Jesus. If the church follows Jesus into death, and even to the hellish places on earth, it is only then that the church will rise again to new life and vibrancy in the Kingdom of God.

Reviews from Amazon

I have often thought on the church and how its acceptance of corporate methods and assimilation of cultural media mores taints its mission but Jeremy Myers eloquently captures in words the true crux of the matter—that the church is not a social club for do-gooders but to disseminate the good news to all the nooks and crannies in the world and particularly and primarily those bastions in the reign of evil. That the "gates of Hell" Jesus pronounces indicate that the church is in an offensive, not defensive, posture as gates are defensive structures.

I must confess that in reading I was inclined to be in agreement as many of the same thinkers that Myers riffs upon have influenced me also—Walter Wink, Robert Farrar Capon, Greg Boyd, NT Wright, etc... So as I read, I frequently nodded my head in agreement. –GN Trifanaff

The book is well written, easy to understand, organized and consistent thoughts. It rightfully makes the reader at least think about things as... is "the way we have always done it" necessarily the Biblical or Christ-like way, or is it in fact very sinful?! I would recommend the book for pastors and church officers; those who have the most moving-and-shaking clout to implement changes, or keep things the same. –Joel M. Wilson

Purchase the eBook for $6.99
Purchase the Paperback for $8.99

Adventures in Fishing (for Men)

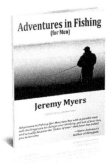

Adventures in Fishing (for Men) is a satirical look at evangelism and church growth strategies.

Using fictional accounts from his attempts to become a world-famous fisherman, Jeremy Myers shows how many of the evangelism and church growth strategies of today do little to actually reach the world for Jesus Christ.

Adventures in Fishing (for Men) pokes fun at some of the popular evangelistic techniques and strategies endorsed and practiced by many Christians in today's churches. The stories in this book show in humorous detail how little we understand the culture that surrounds us or how to properly reach people with the gospel of Jesus Christ. The story also shows how much time, energy, and money goes into evangelism preparation and training with the end result being that churches rarely accomplish any actual evangelism.

Reviews from Amazon

I found *Adventures in Fishing* (*For Men*) quite funny! Jeremy Myers does a great job shining the light on some of the more common practices in Evangelism today. His allegory gently points to the foolishness that is found within a system that takes the preaching of the gospel and tries to reduce it to a simplified formula. A formula that takes what should be an organic, Spirit led experience and turns it into a gospel that is nutritionally benign.

If you have ever EE'd someone you may find Myers' book offensive, but if you have come to the place where you realize that Evangelism isn't a matter of a script and checklists, then you might benefit from this light-hearted peek at Evangelism today. – Jennifer L. Davis

Purchase the eBook for $0.99

Christmas Redemption: Why Christians Should Celebrate a Pagan Holiday

Christmas Redemption looks at some of the symbolism and traditions of Christmas, including gifts, the Christmas tree, and even Santa Claus and shows how all of these can be celebrated and enjoyed by Christians as a true and accurate reflection of the gospel.

Though Christmas used to be a pagan holiday, it has been redeemed by Jesus.

If you have been told that Christmas is a pagan holiday and is based on the Roman festival of Saturnalia, or if you have been told that putting up a Christmas tree is idolatrous, or if you have been told that Santa Claus is Satanic and teaches children to be greedy, then you must read this book! In it, you will learn that all of these Christmas traditions have been redeemed by Jesus and are good and healthy ways of celebrating the truth of the gospel and the grace of Jesus Christ.

Reviews from Amazon

Too many times we as Christians want to condemn nearly everything around us and in so doing become much like the Pharisees and religious leaders that Jesus encountered.

I recommend this book to everyone who has concerns of how and why we celebrate Christmas.

I recommend it to those who do not have any qualms in celebrating but may not know the history of Christmas.

I recommend this book to everyone, no matter who or where you are, no matter your background or beliefs, no matter whether you are young or old. –David H.

Very informative book dealing with the roots of our modern Christmas traditions. The Biblical teaching on redemption is excellent! Highly recommended. –Tamara

Finally, an educated writing about Christmas traditions. I have every book Jeremy Myers has written. His writings are fresh and truthful. –Retlaw "Steadfast"

Purchase the eBook for $3.99

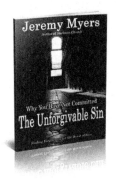

Why You Have not Committed the Unforgivable Sin: Finding Forgiveness for the Worst of Sins

Are you afraid that you have committed the unforgivable sin?

In this book, you will learn what this sin is and why you have not committed it. After surveying the various views about blasphemy against the Holy Spirit and examining Matthew 12:31-32, you will learn what the sin is and how it is committed.

As a result of reading this book, you will gain freedom from the fear of committing the worst of all sins, and learn how much God loves you!

Reviews from Amazon

This book addressed things I have struggled and felt pandered to for years, and helped to bring wholeness to my heart again. – Natalie Fleming

You must read this book. Forgiveness is necessary to see your blessings. So if you purchase this book, [you will have] no regrets. –Virtuous Woman

Jeremy Myers covers this most difficult topic thoroughly and with great compassion. –J. Holland

Good study. Very helpful. A must read. I like this study because it was an in depth study of the scripture. –Rose Knowles

Excellent read and helpful the reader offers hope for all who may be effected by this subject. He includes e-mails from people, [and] is very thorough. –Richie

Purchase the eBook for $5.99
Purchase the Paperback for $5.99

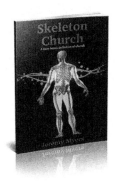

Skeleton Church: A Bare-Bones Definition of Church

The church has a skeleton which is identical in all types of churches. Unity and peace can develop in Christianity if we recognize this skeleton as the simple, bare-bones definition of church. But when we focus on the outer trappings—the skin, hair, and eye color, the clothes, the muscle tone, and other outward appearances—division and strife form within the church.

Let us return to the skeleton church and grow in unity once again.

Reviews from Amazon

My church gathering is struggling to break away from traditions which keep us from following Jesus into the world. Jeremy's book lends encouragement and helpful information to groups like us. –Robert A. White

I worried about buying another book that aimed at reducing things to a simple minimum, but the associations of the author along with the price gave me reason to hope and means to see. I really liked this book. First, because it wasn't identical to what other simple church people are saying. He adds unique elements that are worth reading. Second, the size is small enough to read, think, and pray about without getting lost. –Abel Barba

In *Skeleton Church*, Jeremy Myers makes us rethink church. For Myers, the church isn't a style of worship, a row of pews, or even a building. Instead, the church is the people of God, which provides the basic skeletal structure of the church. The muscles, parts, and flesh of the church are how we carry Jesus' mission into our own neighborhoods in our own unique ways. This eBook will make you see the church differently. –Travis Mamone

This book gets back to the basics of the New Testament church—who we are as Christians and what our perspective should be in the world we live in today. Jeremy cuts away all the institutional layers of a church and gets to the heart of our purpose as Christians in the world we live in and how to affect the people around us with God heart and view in mind. Not a physical church in mind. It was a great book and I have read it twice now. –Vaughn Bender

Purchase the eBook for $3.99

Book Publishing Instructions: A Step-by-Step Guide to Publishing Your Book as a Paperback and eBook

The dirty little secret of the publishing industry is that authors don't really need publishing companies any longer. If you want to get published, you can!

This book gives you everything you need to take your unfinished manuscript and get it into print and into the hands of readers. It shows you how to format your manuscript for printing as a paperback and preparing the files for digital eReaders like the Kindle, iPad, and Nook.

This book provides tips and suggestions for editing and typesetting your book, inserting interior images, designing a book cover, and even marketing your book so that people will buy it and read it. Detailed descriptions of what to do are accompanied by screenshots for each step. Additional tools, tips, and websites are also provided which will help get your book published.

If you have a book idea, you need to read this book.

Reviews from Amazon

I self-published my first book with the "assistance" of a publishing company. In the end I was extremely unhappy for various reasons ... Jeremy Myers' book ... does not try to impress with all kinds of "learned quotations" but gets right to the thrust of things, plain and simple. For me this book will be a constant companion as I work on a considerable list of books on Christian doctrines. Whether you are a new aspiring author or one with a book or so behind you, save yourself much effort and frustration by investing in this book. –Gerrie Malan

This book was incredibly helpful. I am in the process of writing my first book and the info in here has really helped me go into this process with a plan. I now realize how incredibly naive I was about what goes into publishing a book, yet instead of feeling overwhelmed, I now feel prepared for the task. Jeremy has laid out the steps to every aspect of publishing step by step as though they were recipes in a cook book. From writing with Styles and using the Style guide to incorporating images and page layouts, it is all there and will end up saving you hours of time in the editing phase. –W. Rostoll

Purchase the eBook for $9.99
Purchase the Paperback for $14.99

The Lie – A Short Story

When one billion people disappear from earth, what explanation does the president provide? Is he telling the truth, or exposing an age-old lie?

This fictional short story contains his televised speech.

Have you ever wondered what the antichrist will say when a billion people disappear from planet earth at the rapture? Here is a fictional account of what he might say.

Purchase the eBook for $0.99

Printed in Great Britain
by Amazon

45370518R00136